MEDIATING AND NEGOTIATING MARITAL CONFLICTS

For Megan and Theo
D. E.

For Wally, Wendy, Sharon, and Lori
N. S.

MEDIATING AND NEGOTIATING MARITAL CONFLICTS

Desmond Ellis
Noreen Stuckless

SAGE Publications
International Educational and Professional Publisher
Thousand Oaks   London   New Delhi

For information address:

SAGE Publications, Inc.
2455 Teller Road
Thousand Oaks, California 91320
E-mail: order@sagepub.com

SAGE Publications Ltd.
6 Bonhill Street
London EC2A 4PU
United Kingdom

SAGE Publications India Pvt. Ltd.
M-32 Market
Greater Kailash I
New Delhi 110 048 India

Printed in the United States of America

Library of Congress Cataloging-in-Publication Data

Ellis, Desmond.
     Mediating and negotiating marital conflicts / authors, Desmond Ellis,
  Noreen Stuckless.
          p.   cm.
     Includes bibliographical references and index.
     ISBN 0-7619-0502-2 (cloth: acid-free paper). — ISBN 0-7619-0503-0
  (pbk.: acid-free paper).
        1. Divorce mediation.   2. Negotiation.
  3. Marital conflict.
  I. Stuckless, Noreen.   II. Title.
  HQ814.E45   1996
  306.89—dc20   96-10128

This book is printed on acid-free paper.

     97 98 99 10 9 8 7 6 5 4 3 2

Sage Production Editor: Diana E. Axelsen
Sage Typesetter: Marion Warren

Contents

Introduction

Conflicts associated with marital separation and divorce have traditionally been settled by lawyers through negotiations. Since 1980, an increasing proportion of these conflicts have been settled or resolved through the process of marital conflict mediation (Ellis, 1994). Supporters of traditional (adversarial) conflict resolution processes have severely criticized marital conflict mediation for a number of reasons. Two of the most serious of these are its failures to adequately protect women from the violence of their ex-partners and to neutralize the effects of gender-based power imbalances on the agreements that separating women reach with their more powerful male partners. In some critiques, mediators themselves are regarded as the oppresssors. Bush and Folger (1994) include such observations in their summary of the criticisms made against mediation. They refer to these as constituting an "oppression story" (pages 22-24).

Marital conflict mediators and their supporters criticize lawyer negotiations for escalating the conflicts between separating couples and making things worse. Because of this, they allege, women may be at greater risk of being assaulted or otherwise harmed by their ex-partners.

Moreover, they contend that lawyer negotiations are more costly and cause delays that increase stress on separating parents and their children.

A review of these criticisms and counter-criticisms reveals that they are often ideologically driven and rarely supported by empirical research results (Ellis, 1993). The first objective of this book is to add to the corpus of empirically grounded knowledge on the outcomes of negotiation and mediation that began with the publication of Irving and Benjamin's (1984) research in Canada, Pearson and Thoennes's (1984) research in the United States, and the research of Davis (1980a, 1980b) and Davis and Bader (1983) in Britain.

A review of the relevant literature reveals that much of the research on the effects of traditional and alternative marital dispute resolution processes is neither guided by, nor designed to test, theories that explain or account for these effects. Most of the research is practically (problem) oriented. This is as it should be. However, there is no reason why such research should also be "theory-free." The second objective of this book is to stimulate theory-guided, problem-focused research by theorizing about the effects of spousal violence and power imbalances on divorce mediation.

Those who read this book will discover references to "legal aid," "legal aid clients," and "legal aid lawyers." As non-Canadian readers may not be familiar with the Legal Aid Plan in Ontario, the province in which the Family Mediation Pilot Project (Ellis, 1994) was conducted, a brief description is warranted. Ontario's legal aid plan is designed to increase access to justice by using public funds to defray the immediate cost of obtaining legal representation by persons who cannot otherwise afford to do so. There is a means test. Separating-divorcing applicants for legal aid who pass this test are awarded a Legal Aid Certificate (Family). Depending on means or resources, some or all of the cost of this certificate must eventually be repaid. A spouse who is awarded a legal aid certificate can then take it to a lawyer of his or her choice who is in private practice. If the lawyer agrees to represent this person, he or she accepts him or her as a client and submits all bills (disbursements, preparation and court time) to the legal aid plan for payment. The amount of time legal aid lawyers are permitted to spend on any given separation-divorce-related matter is restricted, as is the hourly fee they can charge. Legal aid lawyers then, are regular private practice lawyers who also accept legal aid clients. Their hourly rate of remuneration is lower than it is for regular clients, but their fees are more likely to be paid because it is the government that pays them.

There are 11 chapters in this book. In Chapter 1, major concepts that are referred to in it are defined. These concepts include mediation, negotiation, and power, as well as conflict and control-instigated violence.

Chapter 2 deals with theory. More specifically, it identifies causal mechanisms in lawyer negotiations and mediation that are hypothesized to bring about durable and fair resolutions to conflicts associated with the process of marital separation-divorce.

Conflicts associated with the process of separation-divorce can be resolved through lawyer negotiations or mediation. In Chapter 3, factors influencing the choice of one or the other of these two processes are identified.

The marital histories of separating couples, especially those that include marital violence, may have an effect on the safety of partners who are represented by lawyers as well as those participating in mediation. The risk of violence toward separating partners by their ex-partners during and following their participation in these marital conflict resolution processes varies with the nature and gender patterning of marital violence. These topics are discussed in Chapter 4.

Chapter 5 focuses on postseparation violence. More specifically, the effects of lawyer negotiations and mediation on violence between ex-partners are examined in this chapter.

Power imbalances between separating partners may have an effect on the equity or fairness of agreements reached by mediation participants and the settlements negotiated for their clients by lawyers. Power imbalances between mediators and lawyers and their respective clients also influence the outcomes of mediation and lawyer negotiations. The effects of both types of power imbalances, as well as a process model of power that can be applied to them, are discussed in Chapter 6.

Chapter 7 is devoted to a discussion of the issues that separating partners want mediated or negotiated by their lawyers. Issue-focused outcomes of mediation and negotiations are associated with client satisfaction in rather complex ways. These are identified in Chapter 8.

The outcomes of mediation and lawyer negotiations are included in agreements and minutes of settlement, respectively. Compliance with arrangements set out in agreements and settlements is examined in Chapter 9.

Compliance with some arrangements, child support for example, varies with the economic circumstances of noncustodial parents. The economic condition of separating partners and the economic cost to them of participating in mediation or hiring lawyers to negotiate on their behalf are examined in Chapter 10. In Chapter 11, the final chapter, evidence on the effects of divorce mediation and lawyer negotiations on children's adjustment to divorce is presented and discussed under three subheadings; these are parental conflict, custody arrangements, and income deprivation.

Definitions of Concepts

Conflict-Instigated Abuse

Conflict-instigated abuse refers to acts engaged in by male or female partners with the intention of injuring or hurting their partners, thereby resolving the conflict that motivated the intentional use of the abusive acts in the first place.

This definition builds on the one formulated by Murray Straus (1990). It is relevant to note that the Straus definition deals only with acts and not *injuries*. In this specific sense, it is similar to legal (Criminal Code) definitions of assault. The crime of assault can be injury free. Conflict-instigated abuse is always injury free because the actual infliction of injury or pain is not part of the definition, although it may imply it.

The Conflict Tactics Scale (CTS) is used as one measure of spousal abuse because conflict is associated with the process of separating, and abuse has been found to be associated with conflict. In the Ellis (1994) study, the CTS was not used as the only measure of spousal abuse for two reasons. First, a significant amount of the abuse that male partners direct toward their wives may not be conflict instigated (Dobash,

1

Dobash, Wilson, & Daly, 1992). Second, it provides a misleading account of the patterning of spousal abuse. That is to say, the CTS routinely yields findings indicating that male and female partners are equally likely to abuse each other, not because they really are equally likely to do so but because this instrument itself elicits a symmetrical pattern of responding, and its users equate spousal abuse, generally, with one particular form of abuse: conflict-instigated spousal abuse. By using the CTS as well as other measures of abuse, we are in a position to demonstrate this.

Control-instigated Abuse

Non-conflict-instigated abuse refers to physical, verbal, and emotional abuse as well as the intentional infliction of pain or hurt that is not associated with conflict. A number of feminist writers have defined this form of abuse as *social control motivated*. Social-control-motivated abuse refers to intentionally inflicted physically or psychologically painful or hurtful acts (or threats) by male partners as a means of compelling or constraining the conduct, dress, or demeanor of their female partners. Feminist writers such as Dobash and Dobash (1979) and Hamner (1978) restrict the definition of social-control-motivated abuse to male partners. In the Ellis (1994) study, the definition applies to both male and female partners.

Measures of non-conflict-instigated abuse are used because they uncover a significant amount of abuse that is not revealed by use of the CTS. In addition, they indicate an asymmetrical pattern of abuse that is not shown by the CTS. Third, they include measures that focus on the *consequences* of abuse (e.g., hurting), not on a series of apparently consequence-free acts, as the CTS does. Last, the use of non-conflict-instigated measures, and questions associated with them, provides information on meanings and motives for abuse. The CTS does not.

Costs

Costs are defined as economic costs (as opposed to emotional costs). The personal costs of the mediation service and of lawyer negotiations are defined as the economic costs of clients of providing each mechanism. The public costs of each mechanism refer to the economic costs to the courts.

Dispute Resolution Processes

Adjudication, family mediation, negotiation, and struggle are all mechanisms for resolving and settling disputes or "dealing with opposing preferences" (Carnevale & Pruitt, 1992, p. 532).

Adjudication

Adjudication is a dispute resolution mechanism in which

A third party who is not [herself or] himself directly a disputant . . . holds the legitimate authority and responsibility, to reach and enunciate a decision that is the outcome of the dispute and is . . . [legally] binding on the disputing parties. (Gulliver, 1979, pp. 4-6)

Family mediation

Family mediation is defined as

A voluntary, non-adversarial alternative dispute resolution process in which a third party, the mediator, assists clients of a relatively equal bargaining position reach a mutually satisfactory agreement on issues affecting the family. (Attorney General, 1989, p. 21)

Negotiation

Negotiation is a dispute resolution mechanism in which

Representatives of the disputants whose primary concern is to influence or coerce each other with a view to obtaining an agreement that protects or secures the legal and other expressed interests (preferences) of their own client. (Carnevale & Pruitt, 1992, p. 533)

Struggle

Struggle (interpersonal) is a mechanism in which

The actual or threatened use of physical or emotional injury or deceit is used as a means of winning conflicts or ensuring that the preferences of one of the disputing parties are realized (Carnevale & Pruitt, 1992, p. 252).

In examining the four forms of dispute resolution, it is important to make explicit important differences that are not included in the definitions themselves. Four are noteworthy and relevant to an evaluation of the effects of mediation and the adversarial process on postdivorce outcomes.

Continuum

First, lawyer negotiations in separations and divorces can be placed on a continuum with "highly adversarial" at one end and "highly cooperative-willing to compromise" on the other. Marital conflict mediation can be placed on a continuum with high advocacy for one party at one end and perfect neutrality at the other.

Locus of control

Second, struggle and mediation are forms of dispute resolution in which the parties themselves control the process and outcomes. In negotiation, the parties have some control over their lawyer representatives, but the process itself is mainly under the control of their lawyers. In adjudication, the judge controls both the process and the outcomes.

Threat canopy

Third, both lawyer negotiations and mediation take place under the canopy of adjudication *and,* for women especially, the canopy of struggle. Struggle and adjudication, with their greater costs and risks, including the risk of physical injury, serve as a two-faced threat system. The threat of adjudication coerces separating spouses to settle their differences via negotiation or mediation. The threat of struggle, especially by male spouses in cases where their ex-partners initiated the separation, coerces female ex-partners to accept the preferences or preference orderings of their male ex-partners. These include abandoning the separation and returning to live with them, accepting outcomes they prefer, or both as the price of a struggle-free separation processed by either negotiation or mediation.

Structure and norms

Last, negotiation and mediation differ from each other structurally and normatively. Structurally, the most significant difference is that lawyer negotiations usually involve *dyads* (the two lawyers), whereas mediation usually involves *triads* (the two parties and the mediator). Normatively, mediators give greater weight than lawyers to client control of the process and to outcomes that secure the best interests of the family as a whole.

Effectiveness

Effectiveness refers to the production of individually and socially desired outcomes by marital conflict mediation in comparison with lawyer negotiations. *Ceteris paribus,* the marital dispute resolution mechanism that produces the highest wanted-got ratio and the highest proportion of relatively safe, speedy, satisfying, fair, complied-with, and inexpensive resolutions is the more effective one. Unlike settlements, which represent the termination of the ongoing conflicts, resolutions are settlements or agreements that are lasting, mutually satisfying, and violence free. They also facilitate compliance with the terms set out in them.

Harassment

Harassment refers to persistent, intentional, unwanted, fear-inducing, stressful, or otherwise aversive intrusions that tend to instigate behavior aimed at avoiding harassment. Functionally, harassing acts are similar to hassles in that both instigate avoidance behavior by the target person. Lazarus and DeLongis (1983) define hassles as "the irritating, frustrating, distressing demands and troubled relationships that plague us day in and day out" (p. 243). For these authors, hassles consist of microstressors. The intrusive acts we have defined as harassing acts are conceived of as stressors. The stress and anxiety they induce is greater than the lesser levels of stress induced by hassles. Like Lazarus and DeLongis, we agree that separation-divorce is a major source of stress and brings about "new hassles" (p. 247). Unlike them, we would add harassment to the aversive set of experiences associated with separation-divorce.

Power

Power refers to the ability of parties involved in a conflict to use their resources in ways that bring about a convergence on outcomes they want or desire. The resources available to them (normative and material) define *potential power.* The motivation and ability to use these resources to bring about a desired convergence on outcomes of mediation or negotiation define their *persuasive strength* (power in use).

Power Imbalances

The persuasive strength of parties involved in attempting to resolve marital conflicts (spouses, lawyers, mediators) can be used to bring about convergences on outcomes in which one spouse gains while the other loses, mediators or lawyers gain while one or both spouses lose, or everybody involved loses. In other words, persuasive strength can help bring about positive sum (win-win) as well as zero sum (win-lose) and negative sum (lose-lose) outcomes. Differences in persuasive strength (power imbalances) refer to differences in the resources controlled by the parties to the conflict *and* the motivation and ability to use them to bring about a desired convergence on the outcomes of mediation or negotiation.

Imbalances favoring male partners may be found among couples participating in mediation. This has been commented on by many critics and supporters of mediation. Less frequently noted are imbalances in the power of lawyers hired by male and female ex-partners (Ellis, 1993). Lawyers in any community are ranked according to their ability to win cases for their clients. Male ex-partners are usually in a better financial position. They can afford to hire better lawyers than their female ex-partners. The resulting gender-related imbalances in lawyer power may be reflected in the process and outcomes of lawyer negotiations.

Theory

Causal Mechanisms in Lawyer Negotiations and Mediation

Conflicts associated with marital separation can be settled in a number of ways, including negotiations and third-party intervention. According to Rubin (1994), these are "the two most constructive approaches to the management of conflict" (p. 33). Mediation is a type of third-party intervention. Compared with other approaches, negotiation and mediation are more constructive in two senses. Positively, they contribute more toward reaching mutually satisfactory, durable outcomes, and they generate greater mutual satisfaction with the process itself. They also make a greater contribution toward decreasing the likelihood of negative or harmful outcomes such as violence, domination, and escalation of conflict (Rubin, 1994).[1]

Rubin's two most constructive approaches are not necessarily equally constructive. Indeed, some critics of lawyer negotiations regard them as destructive, and some critics of marital conflict mediation regard this approach as dangerous and unfair to women. These are extreme views. They do emphasize this point, however: There is a great deal of controversy, much of it ideologically motivated, over the relative effectiveness of lawyer negotiations and mediation as ways of resolving marital conflicts.[2]

Our intention in this discussion is not to contribute to extant controversies. Instead, we shall confine our attention to identifying the mechanisms in each process that help explain why and how it brings about constructive resolutions to the conflicts associated with marital separation.[3]

Note that our theoretical focus is on causal mechanisms and not causes. A causal mechanism is any action, reaction, event, process, or character trait that explains why or how the cause "works." Here is an example: The cause of rapid smoothing of the ice surface in a hockey arena is the warm water sprayed on it by a Zamboni machine. The causal mechanism is evaporation.

A more relevant example is cited by Elster (1991). In societies where arranged marriages are the norm and are usual, marrying for love is a cause of unhappy marriages. The causal mechanisms are a character trait, stubbornness, and rejection or social isolation of "deviants" by relatives, friends, and peers (p. 5).

The causal mechanisms we shall identify are drawn from the theoretical formulations of a relatively few contributors to the development of theories regarding lawyer negotiations and mediation, respectively. Without prejudice to the fine work of others, we believe that the contributions of Bush and Folger (1994); Carnevale and Pruitt (1992); Davis (1983); Deutch (1994); Gulliver (1979); Kressel, Frontera, Forlenza, and Butler (1994); and Rubin (1994) are especially significant for our purposes. If we are correct in our judgment, then the theories of lawyer negotiations and mediation we describe ought to be included among the strongest extant versions of them.

At the outset, it should be noted that the legal context in which both lawyer negotiations and mediation operate is one that favors private ordering. That is to say, lawyer negotiators and mediators operate in a context in which they are expected to "facilitate the process by which parties themselves decide what the consequences of divorce should be" (Mnookin, 1979, p. 365). In reality, this expectation (norm) may not be conformed with to an equal degree by lawyers and mediators. Here, following Mnookin, we merely identify the norm or expectation as part of the framework for negotiating and mediating conflicts associated with marital separation.

The reality that both lawyers and mediators confront includes clients who may be, and often are, angry, vengeful, hurt, stressed, and distrustful. They may have been fighting with each other for years before one or both of them attempt to settle their conflicts by separating. Separation itself may have settled some of these conflicts, but it may also have escalated others and created new conflicts. Clearly, mechanisms in lawyer negotiations and mediation that are based on acceptance of the norm of private ordering but that have the effect of dissuading the parties from deciding what the consequences of divorce should be while they are still experiencing high states of emotional arousal will make a positive contribution toward the constructive resolution of conflicts between them.

A Theory of Lawyer Negotiations

Lawyer negotiations can be subsumed under one of two models. *Getting to Yes* is one. *Getting to Why* is the other.[4] These two models stand in an integrative relationship to each other (Rubin, 1994). In practice, a lawyer negotiator may adopt a distributive approach (Getting to Yes) with respect to some issues (e.g., property division) and an integrative approach (Getting to Why) with respect to other issues (e.g., custody and access). Alternatively, he or she may start by adopting a distributive (convergence-concession) approach and later change to an integrative (mutual gains) approach.

The causal mechanisms invoked in the convergence-concession model are aimed at bringing about outcomes that each client wants via relatively speedy settlements. What their clients want drives negotiators in the convergence-concession approach. More specifically, in applying this model, lawyer negotiators inflate the wants of their own clients and the strength of their opposition to giving the other lawyers' clients what they want. Gradually, via a recursive, stepwise process, realistic expectations are communicated. An agreement is reached when one spouse gives the other what he or she wants in return for getting what he or she wants.

Rubin has identified a number of causal mechanisms (he calls them variables) that bring about agreements that one client may want more than the other. The specific causal mechanisms involved include credible commitments, credible threats, and judicious misrepresentation. The first two involve coercion, actual and threatened; the third involves deceit.

For instance, a lawyer negotiator for one spouse can increase the likelihood that the lawyer negotiator for the other spouse will give in or yield in a conflict over financial support if his or her client (say, the husband) deliberately injures himself so that he can no longer work or if he waives his right to a pension by resigning from his job prior to the pension eligibility date.

Yielding can also be made more probable by issuing credible threats. Thus, the lawyer for the spouse with greater financial resources can obtain concessions from the lawyer of the spouse with fewer financial resources by threatening to abandon negotiations for the far more expensive process of litigation.

The likelihood of getting the other spouse's lawyer negotiator to yield can also be increased by judicious misrepresentation. Thus, the chance of paying a smaller monthly amount in child or spousal support payments (what the husband really wants) may be increased if the husband's lawyer tells the wife's lawyer that he is willing to pay any amount requested in child support payments if he has to (which he really ranks highest among the things he does not want to do) but that what he wants most of all is to have sole custody of their two children (which he is really not interested in, but he knows that this is what she wants above all else). Moreover, the husband's lawyer states that his or her client has put in an offer on a larger house so the children can live with him (the lawyer knows that his client intends to withdraw his offer prior to making a binding offer). During the process of negotiations, the husband's lawyer allows himself or herself to be persuaded to yield on custody—to allow the wife to have sole custody of the children—on the condition that she markedly decreases the amount she had formerly demanded in child support.

In the mutual gains (Getting to Why) model, the lawyer negotiator is more concerned with the underlying interests of spouses than with their explicitly stated positions. Moreover, whereas the convergence-concession model is driven by a zero-sum conception of outcomes (one spouse's gain is the other's loss), the mutual gains model is driven by a positive-sum conception of outcomes (both spouses gain).

The causal mechanism linking negotiation with positive-sum outcomes in the mutual gains model is the acquisition of reliable information on the motivations and needs of the spouses. To illustrate the operation of this mechanism, we quote Rubin, who built on an anecdote from the book *Getting to Yes* (Fisher & Ury, 1981).

> Two people are arguing over the division of an orange between them. One asks for an 80-20 split in her favor, to which the other responds with a counteroffer of a 50-50 split, a settlement that appears fair and wise. However, one then proceeds to throw away the peel and eat the fruit . . . while the second throws away the orange and uses the peel to bake a cake. If only the two had discussed *not* how much of the orange each wished to have (or would give up) but *why* each wanted the orange, both would have obtained everything they wanted—instead of throwing out something the other found of value. (Rubin, 1994, p. 27)

Getting to "why," that is, getting to understand the underlying interests of spouses, facilitates reaching durable, mutually satisfactory agreements because negotiation is viewed as a cumulative process: "Through . . . the information exchanged between the partners, each comes to get a better sense of the elements that must be included in an acceptable agreement" (Fisher & Ury, 1981, p. 49).

Obtaining information on the underlying interests of spouses is hard work. It also takes time. By way of contrast, obtaining information on the wants or positions of clients and then making strategic use of this information to win takes less time. The appropriate and judicious mix of strategy, tactics, and hard work maximizes the opportunities family lawyers have to invoke causal mechanisms.

As described here, a theory of lawyer negotiations is one that explains the process as a cause that brings about some outcomes (agreements) in which yielding figures prominently and others in which mutual gains figure prominently. Alternatively, it helps explain why, in any given agreement, yielding figures prominently in settling some issues and mutual gains do so in others.

Mediation[5]

In a recent article, Kressel et al. (1994) identified two models of mediation associated with two different styles of mediation. We shall refer to these as the *problem-solving model* (PSM) and the *settlement-*

orientated model (SOM).[6] Research findings cited by Kressel et al. indicated that the PSM is more likely than the SOM to involve causal mechanisms that link the mediation process (cause) with satisfying durable agreements and greater satisfaction with the mediation process itself (outcomes).

These two models were derived from observation of the mediation of custody and visitation disputes between couples with "extremely high levels of premediation conflicts" (Kressel et al., 1994, p. 70). We believe that the SOM and PSM are more general models, that is, models that can be applied to support and property division disputes as well as custody and access disputes.

As its name implies, the SOM focuses on helping couples reach agreements relatively quickly. The production of agreements per se rather than high-quality, durable agreements is the primary objective. Causal mechanisms producing relatively speedy agreements include client control over the process, mediator neutrality, and an almost exclusive focus on settlements.

A high degree of client control over the process means that mediators are more likely to do what both spouses want. If clients do not want to be asked questions about why they want what they want or questions focused on the underlying causes of their conflicts, mediators will defer to them. On the other hand, if both spouses place a relatively speedy settlement above all other concerns, this is what mediators will aim for. In the short run, spouses get what they want and mediators get high settlement rates.

Mediator neutrality is a causal mechanism because it inhibits mediators from asking either biased or probing questions about underlying interests, even when the participating spouses have not stated a clear preference for a speedy settlement of their disputes. Probing questions may elicit answers that induce the mediator to advocate on behalf of one of the parties (e.g., the wife who has been repeatedly abused by the husband; Davis, 1980a). Advocacy not only violates a professional norm but may also delay or jeopardize the chances of reaching an agreement.

In the PSM, attention is focused on reaching agreements that reflect integrative problem solving. The mediator must work hard and somewhat longer to reach such solutions, and he or she must adopt a leadership role in presenting creative solutions to the spouses.

Causal mechanisms producing integrative solutions include leadership and the sustained quest for information about underlying interests. Specifically, such mutual gains solutions are produced by the thoughtful, persistent, focused probing into extant constraints, underlying interests, and causes of spousal conflicts. The information obtained by a thoughtful, hardworking leader-mediator is the raw material from which creative, integrative solutions are produced. Because of their source, the spouses themselves, and the cognitive contribution of the mediator, integrative agreements are more likely to be reached and to endure.

All of the mechanisms identified here are derived from what Bush and Folger (1994) call the *satisfaction story* (pp. 16-18) of mediation. They contend that the satisfaction story describes mediation in its most widely practiced or paradigmatic form. Facilitating optimal conflict settlements and client satisfaction are the primary objectives of this form of mediation. *The Promise of Mediation* (Bush & Folger, 1994) represents an attempt to replace the satisfaction story with their own "transformation story." The transformation of disputants' characters and facilitating their moral growth are the primary objectives of transformative mediation. Bush and Folger want this kind of mediation to become paradigmatic.

The mechanisms that bring about transformations in character and engender moral growth are empowerment and recognition. *Empowerment* refers to "the restoration to individuals of a sense of their own value and strength and their own capacity to handle life's problems" (Bush & Folger, 1994, p. 2). Self-respect, self-reliance, and self-confidence are all indicators of empowerment. *Recognition* is defined as "acknowledgement and empathy for the situation and problems of others" (p. 2). Empathy and sympathy are indicators of recognition.

Empowerment and recognition are most likely to be inculcated or activated by mediators whose approach is directive in a very subtle way. Mediators who are overtly directive, who persuade disputants to reach agreements that reflect the mediator's conception of a "good agreement" are ignoring the transformative potential of mediation, even though they may be solving disputant problems at a high rate and the solutions are durable.

Evidence indicating that a subtly directive approach focusing on empowerment and recognition is transformative is provided by the case of the sensitive bully. Regis, a middle-aged black man, filed assault charges against Charles, a young black man. Charles was charged with assaulting Regis's thirteen-year-old son, Jerome. Regis and Charles did not know each other, but Charles used to walk through Regis's neighborhood on his way to work and to see his girlfriend, Claudia, who lived in the same neighborhood.

The subtly directive, empowerment-and-recognition-focused mediator opened the session with a description and explanation of the ground rules and the purpose of mediation. Then he asked these questions:

> Why are you here, Regis?
>
> How well do you know Charles?
>
> Why do you think Charles pinned Jerome to the street?
>
> What has taken place since the incident?
>
> What happened, Jerome?
>
> What happened, Charles?
>
> Does Claudia live in Regis's neighborhood?
>
> Charles, apart from Jerome and his friends "saying words to you," did you assault Jerome for any other reasons?
>
> Charles, do you want to say anything more about the words that bothered you so much?
>
> Regis, you attempted to say something while Charles was speaking and I asked to write it down; what is it you wanted to say?
>
> Charles, did you know that Regis had talked to his son Jerome about not being cruel to people?
>
> Charles and Regis, what do you want to happen?

Answers to the mediator's questions revealed that Charles had a severe limp that he was very sensitive about and that the words spoken by Jerome and his friends referred to it. Charles had stated that he was willing to change his route to avoid further problems with Jerome and his friends. Both agreed that Charles would not attack Jerome, Jerome would not call Charles names, Charles would describe his route when visiting Claudia or catching the bus, and that Regis and Charles would contact each other if future problems arose.

For Bush and Folger, this case indicated that during the course of one 90-minute mediation session,

Something had taken place that made any specific agreements unnecessary
. . . [because] these two men came to see each other differently, by recog-
nizing that they were alike—that they both wanted and deserved each
other's acknowledgement or human being (recognition). They were em-
powered because they were aware that they themselves had made decisions
and commitments. (p. 9)

To sum up, the causal mechanisms involved in lawyer negotiations
are (a) credible commitments, (b) credible threats, (c) misrepresentation, and (d) information on underlying interests and causes of conflicts.
The causal mechanisms involved in mediation are (a) client control over
the process; (b) mediator neutrality; (c) a focus on speedy settlements;
(d) mediator leadership; and (e) obtaining information on underlying
interests, motives, needs, and causes of spousal conflicts. In both lawyer
negotiations and mediation, constructive agreements (solutions) are
more likely to be reached when lawyers and mediators include deep,
focused information gathering and creative solutions based on this
information among the causal mechanisms they invoke. Constructive
agreements increase the likelihood of positive postprocessing outcomes
and decrease the probability of negative outcomes, including violence
and harassment.[7] The inculcation or evocation of empowerment and
recognition bring about desirable and durable changes through the
process of transforming individual disputants.

Notes

1. Deutch's (1949) theory of cooperation and competition is a seminal contribution to
contemporary theorizing on negotiations and mediation. His (1994) crude law of social
relations—"the characteristic processes and effects elicited by a given type of social
relationship [cooperative or competitive] also tend to elicit that type of relationship" (p. 15)
is an additional stimulus to theorizing on conflict resolution processes in general.

2. For a review and evaluation, see Ellis (1993).

3. An interesting and erudite account of these mechanisms is provided by Elster (1991,
pp. 3-12).

4. We found Rubin's (1994) references to *Getting to Yes* (Fisher & Ury, 1981) confusing.
To the reader who is not familiar with this book, the title suggests a focus on settlements.
For this reason, we renamed the Fisher and Ury text "Getting to Why" and associate it with
Rubin's mutual gains model of negotiation. We associate the title *Getting to Yes* with his
convergence-concession model.

5. See Folberg and Taylor (1984) for a detailed description of this conflict resolution
process.

6. Kressel et al. (1994) refer to these models as two different types of mediator style.

7. As each of these mechanisms—or more generally, the models in which they are invoked—have certain limitations, we should emphasize their appropriate implementation. In this connection, see also Kressel, Pruitt, and Associates (1989, pp. 405-406) and Rubin (1994, pp. 39-40).

The Choice of Mediation or the Adversarial Process

The decision to participate in mediation or the adversarial process is influenced by a number of factors. Pearson, Thoennes, and Vanderkooi (1982) investigated the effects of three sets of factors on the decision to accept or reject an opportunity to mediate child custody disputes. The first of these was background characteristics. They found that husbands and wives who chose mediation were more highly educated than those who rejected it (65% vs. 53% with graduate school or college degrees), earned higher annual incomes (29% vs. 21%) and were more likely to be employed as professionals or managers (40% vs. 34%). None of these differences are significant. The same thing is true of gender. Specifically, 69% of males (husbands) and 74% of females (wives) chose mediation. Findings reported by Kelly and Gigy (1989) indicate that mediation and adversarial clients differ significantly with respect to age, education, and presence of minor children. More specifically, mediation clients were more highly educated, younger by an average of 3 years, and more likely to have children under the age of 18. The combined median income of clients in both groups was similar (approximately $59,000).

Kelly and Gigy (1989) also reported findings on the reasons given by mediation clients for choosing mediation. Four reasons identified by more than 80% of male and female partners are to (a) reach an agreement that is satisfactory to both of us (93%), (b) reduce or avoid hostility between us (83%), (c) reduce the cost of obtaining a lawyer (82%), and (d) reduce involvement with lawyers and court proceedings (81%). Overall, men were more positive about starting mediation than women.

Separating or divorcing spouses who participated in the adversarial process chose lawyers to represent them for a number of reasons (Bantz, 1991). Among men, three of the most important of these were "[I] wanted child custody, [I] wanted an expert to handle [the divorce]," and "my spouse hired an attorney so I had to hire one, too" (Hillary & Johnson, 1985, p. 98). Among women, the three most important reasons were "[I] wanted physical child custody, [I] wanted an attorney to help negotiate child support," and "my spouse and I had a lot of property to divide" (p. 98). Compared with men, women attributed more importance to child custody and child support reasons.

"Marital and divorce experiences" was the second set of factors investigated by Pearson et al. (1992). They found that acceptors (those who accepted mediation) were more ambivalent than rejectors (those who rejected mediation) about getting a divorce (20% vs. 14%).[1] This difference is not significant. There was a highly significant difference, however, between the proportion of acceptors and rejectors who reported "no communication" (15% vs. 52%). Gender differences with respect to these two factors are not significant, or where they are significant (e.g., no communication and reject mediation), the numbers involved are too small to yield a reliable finding.

Kelly and Gigy (1989) also reported finding no significant differences in "some of the central marital and relationship variables expected to discriminate between mediation and adversarial respondents" (p. 269). Specifically, they found no significant differences between members of these two groups on divorce-specific anger, amount of marital conflict during the 2 years preceding separation, nonmutuality in the decision to divorce, poor cooperation, or poor communication. "Sampling differences" is the reason given by Kelly and Gigy for the finding that communication is a significant discriminator in the 1992 Pearson et al. study but not in theirs. To this, we would add differences in the proportion of clients for whom custody was an issue in the child custody mediation (Pearson et al.) and Kelly and Gigy's comprehensive mediation samples.

Pearson et al. (1992) also reported another significant difference between husbands and wives. This is the proportion who reported rejecting mediation because of "mistrust or fear of spouse" (10% vs. 28%). Spousal violence may have been responsible for the fear reported by women, but it is not included among the list of marital and divorce experience factors identified by Pearson et al.[2] Ellis (1994), however, did include it among his predictors of choice of mediation or lawyer negotiations by participants in the Family Mediation Pilot Project.

The set of findings we shall describe is based on the analysis of subsamples of wives and husbands. We start with wives.

Eight variables were entered in the predictive model for wives. These are the following:

Sex

Physical, emotional, or verbal abuse and abuse as a major reason for separating

Duration of separation

Level of education

Poor communication as a major reason for separating

Conflict-instigated violence scale score

Total control-instigated violence (the scale included physical, verbal, and emotional abuse)

Monthly income

Of the eight variables loaded in the model, two were statistically significant predictors of choice of lawyer or mediator by wives in the sample. These were monthly income and level of education. Together with findings generated by cross-tabulations, these results indicate that wives earning less than $2,000 a month and who had not graduated from high school were overrepresented among wives who engaged lawyers.

The same eight variables entered in the predictive model for wives were also included in the predictive model for husbands. Of these eight variables, two—monthly income and duration of separation—were statistically significant predictors of choice of lawyer or mediator by male clients (Ellis, 1994). When combined with the results of cross-tabulations, these findings suggest that males earning $2,000 or more in monthly earnings and who have been separated for less than 2 years are overrepresented among male clients participating in mediation.

The choice of lawyer negotiations or mediation is also influenced by spousal violence. For the total sample, evidence cited in Ellis (1994) shows the association between all of the instrumental hurting measures and choice of lawyer or mediator to be statistically significant. For two of the three measures of control-instigated violence, the direction of the association is the same: A significantly higher proportion of clients who reported these forms of abuse chose mediation. A higher proportion of more recently abused clients chose lawyers.

The association between each of the two measures of control-instigated violence (minor and serious) and choice of lawyer or mediator is not statistically significant. Conflict-instigated violence then, does not have a significant effect on the choice of either lawyer negotiations or mediation (Ellis, 1994).

Among females (wives) and males (husbands), only one of the five measures of abuse included for the total sample was associated with choice of lawyer or mediator. Table 3.1 shows a statistically significant association between recent abuse—that is, abuse occurring during the 6 months prior to separation—and choice of lawyer negotiations or mediation by wives and husbands. The direction of the association however, is different for wives and husbands. Among wives, a significantly higher proportion who reported being subject to control-instigated violence by their ex-partners chose lawyers. Among husbands who reported the same experiences, a higher proportion chose mediators.

The third set of factors investigated by Pearson et al. (1992) comprised reactions to the adversarial process. Among those who accepted mediation, relatively high proportions did not have joint custody (71%), were dissatisfied with the court (61%), had participated in counseling (60%), or believed that judges were biased against fathers (56%). Significant differences between husbands and wives were found for the belief that judges were biased against fathers. Among those who rejected mediation, 52% had received counseling, 48% were dissatisfied with the court, 34% did not have joint custody, and 33% believed that judges were biased against fathers.

Table 3.1 Choice of Lawyer Negotiations or Mediation by Spousal Abuse for Total and Wives and Husbands Samples

Dependent Variables	Sample	n	Independent Variables	χ^2	df	Significance
Choice of lawyer or mediator	Total	331	Serious abuse per the Conflict Tactics Scale	.76	1	ns[a]
		308	Minor abuse per the Conflict Tactics Scale	.81	1	ns
		331	Intentional hurt, ever	7.71	1	***
		358	Total Control Abuse Index[b]	12.62	1	***
		323	Recent abuse[c]	16.82	1	***
	Wives	224	Recent abuse	3.85	1	*
	Husbands	96	Recent abuse	5.0	1	*

a. ns = not significant.
b. The Total Control Abuse Index is made up of these items: (a) physical, emotional, or verbal hurting during the 6 months prior to separation for any reason not connected with an ongoing conflict, (b) ex-partner intentionally hurt you, ever, and (c) ex-partner's abuse a major reason for separating.
c. This refers to the first item included in the Total Control Abuse Index: abuse experienced during the 6 months prior to separating.
* $p<.01$; *** $p<.001$.

Pearson et al. (1992) also found significant differences in the gender patterning of reasons for the decision to accept or reject mediation. Among husbands, the greatest differences between those who accepted and rejected mediation were found for these three reasons: no joint custody, 54% (77% accepted vs. 23% rejected); belief that judges were biased, 50% (83% accepted vs. 33% rejected); and a lawyer encouraged mediation, 36% (66% accepted vs. 32% rejected). Among wives, the greatest differences were found for the lawyer-encouraged mediation, 54% (72% accepted vs. 18% rejected); have sole custody, 40% (70% accepted vs. 30% rejected); and the belief that judges were biased against fathers (33% accepted vs. 0%).

Most of the differences reported here are in the same direction for husbands and wives. That is to say, the differences always favor acceptors. A different pattern is revealed, however, when findings on perceived chances of winning in court are presented. This is a significant reason for deciding to accept or reject mediation, but it is not one of the top three reasons. Among husbands, 32% of those who believe their chances of winning in court are 90% or better rejected mediation and only 13% accepted it, a difference of 19% favoring rejectors. Among wives, the comparable figures are 49% and 43%, a difference of 6% favoring acceptors. Clearly, win-lose considerations exert a greater influence on the decision to accept or reject mediation by husbands.

Among husbands then, not having joint custody most effectively discriminates among those who accept or reject mediation followed by belief that judges are biased against fathers, lawyer-encouraged mediation, and win-lose considerations. Among wives, lawyer-encouraged mediation is followed by sole custody and belief that judges are biased against fathers. Among husbands and wives, lawyer-encouraged mediation most effectively discriminates between acceptors and rejectors. For Pearson et al. (1992), it is "the key reason why men and women choose to mediate" (p. 29). This finding is supported by the research of Ellis (1994).

To a significant degree, the choices of clients in the mediation and adversarial samples were influenced by the information provided by lawyers about the law, "lawyering," and mediation, and by mediators about the law, mediation, and lawyering. The starting point for the Ellis (1994) investigation was the law.

Shadow of the Law

The law, in the books and in practice, constitutes one important set of constraints and opportunities. Specifically, the legal context in which such choices are made include the Divorce Act (1985), the Family Law Act (1990), and the Children's Law Reform Act (1990). The Divorce Act (Subsec. 9) states the following:

> (2) It is the duty of every barrister, solicitor, lawyer or advocate who undertakes to act on behalf of a spouse in a divorce proceeding to discuss with the spouse the advisability of negotiating the matters that may be the subject of a support order or a custody order and to inform the spouse of

the mediation facilities known to him or her that might be able to assist the spouse in negotiating those matters.

(3) Every document presented to a court by a barrister, lawyer or advocate that formally commences a divorce proceeding shall contain a statement by him or her certifying that he or she has complied with this section.

Clearly, in the context of divorce proceedings, law in the books places a duty on a lawyer to provide a framework for choice that includes mediation when matters relating to support or custody are involved. Clients who have been informed about the availability of mediation and who decide not to participate in this process have, we may tentatively conclude, voluntarily chosen lawyer negotiations. Clients who were not told about mediation services have, by this omission, been gently pushed into lawyer negotiations.

The Children's Law Reform Act (Sec. 10 (6)) states this:

31(1) Upon an application for custody of or access to a child, the court at the request of the parties, by order may appoint a person selected by the parties to mediate any matter specified in that order.

The duty placed on the court by law is restricted to matters relating to custody and access.[3] With respect to these matters, a judge can order the appointment of a mediator selected by the parties when the parties themselves have requested mediation. Because relatively few separating couples know enough about mediation to make an informed request, and even fewer know the mediator they may wish to select, their requests and selections may follow rather than precede the judge's order. To the extent that this is true, couples referred to mediation by the courts may see themselves not as volunteers but as couples who are being pushed toward participation in this process.

Of the 361 clients sampled, 192 (53.1%) were lawyer clients and 169 (46.8%) were clients of mediators. Actually participating in mediation or lawyer negotiations does not necessarily represent the best way clients in the lawyer and mediation samples thought their marital conflicts could be settled. Table 3.2 shows that almost two thirds (65.9%) of the mediation clients participated in a marital conflict resolution process they judged to be the best way for them. The corresponding proportion for clients in the lawyer sample was less than

Table 3.2 Ways of Settling Marital Conflicts: Preferences and
Aversions of Lawyer and Mediation Clients (by percentage)

Preferences and Aversions	Mediator (n = 169)		Lawyer (n = 192)		Their Own
	Face to Face	Separate[a]	Face to Face[b]	Separate[c]	Face to Face
Best Way					
Lawyer clients	8.9	0.5	17.2	48.4	21.9
Mediator clients	65.9	9.4	1.2	4.2	4.7
Worst Way					
Lawyer clients	1.0	0.5	5.2	28.1	58.3
Mediator clients	1.2	0.6	35.3	35.3	36.5

NOTE: Figures were produced by answers to the following question: Couples who are separating settle differences about property, financial support, custody of children, and access to children in different ways. These include the five ways listed below. Which of these would be best and worst for you? Also, row totals do not sum to 100% because missing cases have been excluded.
a. This term refers to "shuttle" mediation where the mediator talks to each spouse separately, alternating sessions from one to the other.
b. This refers to the presence of both spouses and their lawyers at the meeting(s).
c. This refers to the usual situation in which the spouses' lawyers negotiate with each other.

half (48.4%). Compared with lawyer clients then, a higher proportion of mediation clients were participating in a process that they thought was the best way for them to settle their marital conflicts.

The patterning of lawyer and mediator client aversions was also quite different. Well over half (58.3%) of the lawyer clients thought face-to-face meetings "on our own" was the worst way of settling their marital conflicts. More than one quarter (28.1%) felt the same way about "separate meetings with lawyers." The aversions of mediation clients were more evenly divided between these two contexts. Specifically, just over one third of them (36.5%) thought "on our own, face to face" was the worst way, and slightly more than one third (35.3%) thought that "separate meetings with lawyers" was the worst way of settling their conflicts.

When the modal (most frequent) "best way" and "worst way" attributions by lawyer and mediator clients were compared, we discovered far greater consistency among the attributions of mediator clients. Thus,

Table 3.2 shows that 65.9% of mediator clients thought that mediation was the best way of settling their marital conflicts. The corresponding figures for lawyer clients are 48.4% and 28.1%. Compared with lawyer clients, a higher proportion of mediator clients felt that their choice of marital conflict resolution process was the best way for them to settle their conflicts. Conversely, compared with lawyer clients, a far smaller proportion of mediation clients thought their choice of mediation was the worst way of settling their conflicts (1.2% vs. 28.1%).

To sum up, findings presented in Table 3.2 indicate that more than one quarter (i.e., 28.1%) of the lawyer clients were participating in a marital conflict resolution process that they thought was the worst way of settling their conflicts. Under one half (48.4%) were participating in a process that they thought was the best way of settling their conflicts. A far smaller proportion (1.2%) of mediation clients thought they were participating in a process that was the worst way of settling their marital conflicts. A markedly higher proportion of them (65.9%) were participating in a process that they thought was the best way of settling their conflicts.

The relatively close correspondence between the actual and best choices of mediation clients was due in part to the steps taken by judges and mediators in the Hamilton Unified Family Court [Ontario] to ensure that the choice of mediation is truly voluntary. First of all, communication between judges and mediators helps create a situation in which judges refer rather than order couples to mediation.

Second, both parties are contacted by telephone within five days of a referral. During these conversations, the willingness and readiness of both parties to participate in mediation is ascertained. Then, both parties are presented with the opportunity to attend a family law information meeting prior to entry into mediation. Spouses are urged to attend separate meetings (see Figure 3.1 at the end of this chapter). At the meeting, mediation and lawyer options are described, and questions raised by spouses are answered. Last, at intake, each party is interviewed individually to confirm both the choice and the feasibility of mediation.

The relative lack of correspondence between the actual and the best choices of lawyer clients may be due in part to the clients' relatively low level of education and in part to the fact that approximately half of the lawyer clients did not know very much about the specific lawyer they engaged. In addition, most of the lawyer clients in the sample reported that they were not informed of the mediation option by their lawyers. It seems that relatively few lawyer clients made fully informed choices of either their lawyer or the marital conflict resolution process they selected.

In this connection, two representative comments are relevant. When asked why he had chosen a lawyer to process his separation, a male lawyer client replied, "What the hell else is there?" A female lawyer client provided this answer to the same question: "There is no other way."

For the lawyer client sample as a whole, just over one quarter (28.1%) reported that their lawyers had informed them about mediation facilities. Qualitative data included in the questionnaire and interviews with mediators indicate that in approximately 4% of these cases, information on the availability of mediation was given to clients only after they had run out of money. In the vernacular of the matrimonial law workers, these clients were dumped by their lawyers. Among this group were some clients who had already been dumped by their ex-partners. They were more than a little put off at being dumped twice.

Compared with their male ex-partners, female clients of lawyers appeared to be less likely to be informed about mediation facilities. Thus, only about one quarter of female lawyer clients (26.6%), but more than one third (37.1%) of male lawyer clients, reported being informed about mediation facilities by their lawyers.

Lawyer clients were also asked whether they had obtained information from any source about the lawyer they chose prior to making their choice. Approximately half (48%) of the clients in the total lawyer sample (48% in the female subsample and 51% in the male subsample) reported having obtained some prior information. Analysis of the qualitative data indicates that the quality and the quantity of information obtained varied greatly. Approximately 44% of the total lawyer client sample (45% females and 40% males) reported having obtained no prior information about the lawyer they eventually chose to represent them. In sum, relatively few lawyer clients made fully informed choices of either their lawyer or the lawyer-controlled process they selected.

Summary of Findings

Compared with clients who chose mediation, clients who chose lawyer negotiations were poorer, less well educated, had been separated for a longer period of time, and had been more recently abused by their partners.

Choice of marital dispute resolution process varies with gender, with females being more likely to choose lawyer negotiations and males being more likely to choose mediation.

Compared with clients in the lawyer sample, a significantly higher proportion of clients in the mediation sample were participating in a process that they believed was the best way for them to settle issues associated with their separation (65.9% vs. 48.4%).

Compared with mediation clients, a significantly higher proportion of clients in the lawyer sample were participating in a process that they believed was the worst way for them to settle issues associated with their separation (28.1% vs. 1.2%).

Compared with lawyer clients, a significantly higher proportion of choices made by mediation clients were more informed choices (100% vs. 44.0%).

Conclusions

▓ The choices of mediation clients are more fully informed than those of lawyer clients.

▓ Lawyers are doing a poor job of informing their clients about the mediation options open to them.

▓ Recency of abuse influences the choice of marital resolution process.

Notes

1. For a more general discussion of the roles of *dumper* and *dumped,* see Hopper (1992).

2. Kelly and Gigy (1989) investigate the effect of anger and conflict on the choice of mediation or the adversarial process, but like Pearson and her associates (1992), they do not identify the contribution made by spousal violence to the choice of one or the other of these processes.

3. The Family Law Act states the following:

3(1) Mediation—In an application under this Act, the court may, on motion, appoint a person whom the parties have selected, to mediate any matter that the court specifies. Note too, that matters relating to support are governed by this Act. This Act deals with matters relating to support.

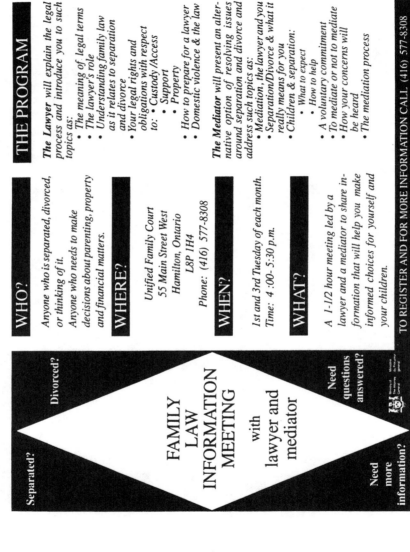

Figure 3.1. Family Law Information Meeting Flyer

Marital Violence

Family mediators often attempt to facilitate the settlement of conflicts between partners whose marital histories include partner violence. The same thing is true of lawyers who attempt to negotiate settlements for their clients. Lawyers and mediators should be aware of violence in the marital histories of their clients for at least three good reasons. The first has to do with their safety. Partners who have assaulted and emotionally abused their partners during their marital relationship are most likely to assault or abuse them during and following negotiations or mediation (Monahan, 1981; O'Leary, 1993).

Second, the possession of greater "harm resources" by one partner (e.g., physical strength, credible threats, stock of swear words and demeaning utterances) combined with a greater willingness to use them against the other, may cast a coercive shadow over the processes of mediation and negotiation, exacerbate conflicts associated with separation, or both. In the former case, the capacity of the harmed partners to bargain as equals (mediation) or to adequately instruct their surrogate bargainers (lawyer negotiators) may be impaired. In the latter case, harmed partners may use the dispute resolution process as a means of getting back at or harming their former assailants. In the process, their children may also suffer.

Third, a significant proportion of lawyer and mediation clients reported being the victims of partner violence. Thus, in Ellis's (1994) study, "partner's physical/emotional abuse as a major reason for separating" was cited by 61% of wives ($n = 247$) and 31% of husbands ($n = 112$).

In addition to implementing explicit steps to obtain information about violence in the marital histories of their clients, lawyers and mediators can also help make their respective dispute resolution processes safer and fairer by acquiring systematic and reliable information on marital violence in general. Specific information provided by individual clients could then be interpreted in the light of more general information that can serve as a context or caveat for violence in individual cases.

Marital violence in society varies along a number of dimensions that are relevant to the processes of mediation and lawyer negotiations. Two of these are singled out for comment. They are (a) types of violence and violent partners and (b) the gender patterning of violence. Conceptions and definitions of violence and violent partners, as well as findings on the gender patterning of spousal violence, vary with two major approaches to the study of spousal violence. One approach (family violence) is consistent with mediation. The other approach (violence against women), is consistent with lawyering in the context of an adversarial system. It is with a brief description of these two approaches that we begin our exposition.[1]

Family Violence Approach

The family violence approach is characterized by the application of systems theory to the problem of explaining family violence. Straus (1973) and Giles-Sims (1983) are two of its most frequently cited advocates. As a social system, the family is made up of family members who are simultaneously dependent on each other (interdependent) and also relatively independent (autonomous) of each other. Being interdependent means that a change in one member's condition or conduct will lead to changes in the condition or conduct of others, which in turn will influence the conduct of the members who originated the interaction. Because the effects of interaction are recursive, causal mechanisms are necessarily circular.

Second, the family system is not only a recursive (feedback or mutual influence) system, it is also conceived of as a relatively closed system. That is to say, in explaining violent or other types of family interaction, factors and influences operating within the family are emphasized. Relatively little weight is given to external (societal) factors that may influence family interaction either directly or indirectly.

Third, the family system, rather than pathological individuals, is regarded as the overriding cause of violent or other types of family interaction.

Fourth, conflict is viewed as endemic in the family system. The roots of conflict may be traced to the admixture of love-hate in intimate, erotic relationships (Freud, 1948; Simmel, 1955) and the attempts by individual family members to maintain or expand their autonomy. Family members who are living together also have more opportunities for becoming involved in conflicts. Last, the precipitators of conflicts are more numerous in families than in other social settings because family resources, which are almost always scarce relative to the demands for them by family members, cover a broader range of material and psychic wants (e.g., attention, affection, money, television shows, use of the car, clothing, etc.).

Fifth, conflicts in all families coexist with tactics of resolving them. Violence is conceived as one of a number of tactics of conflict resolution. Because family members are interdependent and conflict refers to a particular kind of relationship between two or more of them, the tactics used by one member influence the tactics used by the other, which in turn influence the tactics chosen by the first. In this mutual influence process, there are no clearly defined victims or perpetrators, only family members who are attempting to resolve conflicts by reliance on violent tactics. The conception of violence as a tactic of conflict resolution requires that violence between family members be measured by the Conflict Tactics Scale (Straus, 1990).

Last, the family violence approach is applicable to all forms of family violence (i.e., spousal abuse, child abuse, and elder abuse).

Compatibility With Mediation

The theoretical underpinnings of the family violence approach and mediation are alleged to be similar. Thus, family systems theory is definitive of the former, whereas the latter has "significant roots" in it (Kressel, Butler-DeFreitas, Forlenza, & Wilcox, 1989). Family systems theorists invite or require family mediators to do the following:

View the family as a closed system (i.e., one that is immune from outside influences)[2]

Focus on interaction

Focus on future behavior

Attribute joint responsibility for violence (i.e., avoid classifying partners as perpetrators and victims)

Refer to couples therapy, if this is called for (e.g., couples who wish to reconcile)

Focus on the family as a whole (i.e., both partners and the children)

Facilitate the learning of nonviolent, positive-sum ways of settling conflicts (e.g., via compromise)

Focus on differentiation of family roles, not their hierarchal organization with respect to social power

View family violence as a tactic of conflict resolution

Violence Against Women Approach

The violence against women approach is characterized by the application of theories in which gender and power are central to the problem of explaining male violence toward women in general and male violence toward their intimate female partners in particular. Dobash and Dobash (1979, 1992) and Yllö (1993) are two of its well-known feminist advocates.[3] In their explanations, males use their structural position of dominance in society to socially construct the gender roles of male and female in ways that help maintain male dominance over females.

Second, the family is viewed as an open system. That is to say, it is open to societal influences in general and gendered influences in particular. Male-dominated families reflect male dominance in the wider society.

Third, the motivation of male partners to maintain or extend control over their female partners is the overriding cause of male violence toward them.

Fourth, male violence toward women is conceived of as a means of social control. The family violence theorist's conception of male and female partner violence as a factor of conflict resolution is flatly rejected.

Fifth, the conception of male violence toward women as a means of social control requires that violence toward female partners by male partners be measured by questions that focus on violence as an instrument of social control.

Compatibility With Lawyering[4]

The theoretical assumption of lawyers negotiating, prosecuting, and defending in the context of an adversarial system as well as those adopting a violence toward women approach are similar in that both take adversarial relations as given. Violence toward women theorists invite or require family lawyers to do the following:

View the family as an open system

Focus on culpable action

Focus on past behavior

Attribute sole responsibility for violence to perpetrators

Focus on clients and act as advocates for them

Use criminal justice and matrimonial justice system measures to protect women and deter male perpetrators by punishing them

Focus on differences in power resources possessed by male and female partners

View male violence toward female partners as a means of social control

Marital Violence: Definitions

Family violence researchers, such as Straus and Gelles (1990), define violence as "an act carried out with the intention or perceived intention of physically hurting another person" (p. 21). We expand this definition to include psychologically hurting another person (i.e., by demeaning them, calling them names). This expanded definition would appear to make it acceptable to violence against women theorists such as Yllö (1993).[5]

Conceptions: Conflict-Instigated, Control-Instigated, and Anger-Instigated Violence

A review of the general literature on violence and aggression, as well as the literature on spousal violence in particular, reveals the existence of three major conceptions of violence. These are conflict-instigated, control-instigated, and anger-instigated violence.

A conception of conflict-instigated violence is formulated by proponents of the family violence approach (e.g., Straus, 1990). They conceive of violence between spouses as a tactic of conflict resolution.

A conception of control-instigated violence is offered by advocates of the violence against women approach (e.g., Dobash & Dobash, 1992; Hamner & Maynard, 1987; Yllö, 1993). They conceive of male violence as a means of social control, and they believe that the male partner's motivation to maintain or extend control over his female partner is the major source of male violence toward intimate female partners.

A conception of anger-instigated violence tends to be ignored by advocates of both the family violence and violence against women approaches. Psychologist Leonard Berkowitz (1978, 1982, 1993), a leading student of violent behavior, has formulated a conception of angry aggression or violence as an explosive emotional outburst. Angry aggression can often appear to occur out of the blue.[6] Actually, it is preceded by or linked with the experience or perceived experience of an aversive event(s) by the aggressor and is aimed only at injuring the target (Berkowitz, 1993).

For Berkowitz, anger associated with the experience of aversive events is one source of male violence toward female partners. He would readily concede that male partners also hurt their female partners for instrumental reasons having to do with resolving conflicts or maintaining control. Because all three types of violence coexist, they should all be separately measured even though they may be intermingled behaviorally.[7]

Violent Partners: Types

Based on their studies of 140 high-conflict families in child custody disputes who were referred for counseling and mediation by local family courts, Johnston and Campbell (1994) generated four types of violent partners. These, together with their associated power dynamics, modal types of violence, violence severity, and risk of postseparation risk of violence, are presented in Table 4.1.

The typology presented by Johnston and Campbell (1994) may be especially inviting to mediators because it was inductively derived from evidence provided by couples whose conflicts were being mediated. At the same time, caution should be exercised with respect to three issues. First, there is some overlap among the four types of violent partners. Second, the evidence we have examined indicates that male partners are far more likely than female partners to be assailants after separation (Dobash, Dobash, Wilson, & Daly, 1992; Ellis & Wight, 1995; Mahoney, 1991). Third, their typology does not explicitly identify a very dangerous type of male violent partner, the generally violent type.

General aggressors, family-only aggressors, and *emotionally volatile aggressors* are three types of violent male partners identified by Saunders (1992). These subtypes were derived by analyses of two sources of data. First, he performed a cluster analysis on self-report data provided by 165 males participating in treatment programs for wife abuse. Then, he obtained information on 10 other (external) variables, such as childhood abuse and arrests for drunk driving. The three subtypes emerged when he compared the clusters with the external variables. These are presented in Table 4.2.

Table 4.2 shows that general aggressors inflict the most severe violence on their female partners. Not shown in this table are these findings: Most of them have criminal records and the most traditional (conservative) sex role beliefs. Compared with those in the other two groups, family-only aggressors reported the most liberal sex role beliefs. Also notable is the fact that other evidence suggests that Saunders may have underestimated the proportion of family-only batterers who engage in anger-instigated violence (Dutton & Browning, 1988; Faulk, 1974; Hershon & Rosenbaum, 1991; Margolin, Sibner, & Gleberman, 1988).

(text continued on p. 38)

Table 4.1 Types of Violent Marital Partners by Power Dynamics, Severity of Violence, and Postseparation Risk of Violence

Violent Partner Type	Gender	Type of Violence	Power Dynamics	Severity of Violence	Postseparation Risk of Violence
Ongoing episodic assaulter	Male	Control or anger instigated	Male partner dominant	Very high	High
Reactive, explosive assaulter	Female	Anger instigated	Female partner dominant	Very low	Low
Interactive assaulter	Male or female	Conflict instigated	Male partner dominance variable	Variable: very high to low	Low
Separation assaulter	Male or female	Control or anger instigated	"Dumped" partner dependent or "dumper" has challenged dominance of former partner by separating	Lethal to high	High

SOURCE: Adapted from Johnston and Campbell (1993).

36

Table 4.2 Three Types of Violent Male Partners

Type	Percentage	Marital Conflict	Alcohol Level	Anger Level	Abused as Children	Severity of Violence	Type of Violence [a]
General aggressor	29.0	Frequent	Most of the time	Moderate	Most	Most severe	Control and conflict instigated
Family-only aggressor	52.0	Infrequent	Half the time	Low	Some	Least severe	Control instigated
Emotionally volatile aggressor	19.0	Very frequent	Rarely	Very high	Many	Moderately severe	Anger instigated

SOURCE: Adapted from Saunders (1993).

a. Types of violence were not identified by Saunders. We have included them on the basis of protocols cited by Saunders and others who have done research on males entering programs for batterers (e.g., Hamberger & Hastings, 1985; Holtzworth-Munroe, 1994).

Using information obtained from three samples of abused women, Gondolf (1988) and Gondolf and Fisher (1988) were able to identify three main types (clusters) of male batterers.

Two of the male batterer subtypes identified by these researchers were *sociopathic batterers* (5% to 8%) and *antisocial batterers* (30% to 42%). These were the most violent subtypes in terms of the frequency and severity of their violent acts. They may be subsumed under Saunders's general aggressors type. A word of caution is warranted, however: A relatively small subset of general aggressors (sociopathic batterers) poses by far the greatest risk of serious injuries to intimate female partners.

The third subtype, identified by Gondolf and Fisher (1988), is called *typical batterers* (50%). These batterers were more likely to engage in less severe forms of violence. Also, compared with sociopathic and antisocial batterers, they were far less likely to blame their partners.

The research of Saunders (1993), Gondolph (1988), and Gondolf and Fisher (1988), as well as male batterer typologies published by 13 other researchers, was reviewed by Holtzworth-Monroe and Stuart (1994). Based on this evidence, they formulated a developmental model of marital violence featuring three types of male batterers. These are *generally violent-antisocial, family only,* and *dysphoric-borderline.* There is considerable overlap between these types and those identified by Saunders, Gondolph, and Gondolph and Fisher. The consistency between their typologies is noteworthy, considering the differences in approach (rational-deductive and empirical-inductive) and the 20-year period during which the studies were conducted. Moreover, the large number of subjects who were studied—more than 2,000 male batterers and female victims—yields relatively stable findings.

The types of violent partners presented in Tables 4.1 and 4.2 may be stable, but they are also open to the criticism that they present an inaccurate description of the gender patterning of spousal violence. After all, violent female partners were included among the subjects sampled in only one of the studies (Johnston & Campbell, 1993), and the proportion of female partners classified as *female initiators* was not revealed. Moreover, when female victims of male partner violence were included in samples (e.g., Gondolf & Fisher, 1988), they were not asked to report on their own violent behavior. Finally, when male batterers were sampled, they were not asked about the violence directed toward them by their female partners. There may have been good reasons for

not asking these questions, but the end result is that evidence on the
violent spouse types presented here cannot be used as a basis for drawing
valid conclusions about the gender patterning of spousal violence. We
shall have to look elsewhere for this.

[handwritten margin note: In Ird. female initiators many.]

The Gender Patterning of Spousal Violence

The gender patterning of spousal violence refers to the relative
frequencies with which male and female partners hit or abuse their
partners and the comparative seriousness of the injuries they inflict on
each other (Ellis & Dekeseredy, 1995; Ellis & Wight, 1995). Table 4.3
presents the results of a review of all surveys of spousal violence
published in Canada during the years 1981 to 1994. This table reveals
that one measure, the conflict tactics scale (CTS), dominates research
on spousal violence. Thus, conflict-instigated and control-instigated
violence was measured in only one of the nine surveys on nonlethal
violence (Ellis, 1994). Table 4.3 also reveals that the single spousal
homicide survey and only three of nine surveys on nonlethal spousal
violence reported findings on both male and female partner victims.
What do these four surveys reveal about the gender patterning of
spousal violence?

First of all, by a ratio of 3 to 1, wives are more likely to be killed by
their husbands than vice versa (Wilson & Daly, 1994). A similar asymmetrical pattern is reported for spousal homicides committed over a
19-year period in Ontario, Canada (Crawford & Gartner, 1992). In the
United States, the pattern of spousal homicides is symmetrical. That is
to say, an approximately equal number of males and females kill their
partners. However, this is largely an artifact of the markedly higher rate
of homicide among African Americans *and* a gender pattern in which
131 female partners kill male partners for every 100 male partners who
kill their female partners.[8] In most Western, highly technologized societies for which we have spousal homicide data, more males kill their
female partners than vice versa.[9]

Somer's (1992, 1994) findings led to an erroneous conclusion about
the gender patterning of spousal violence for the following reasons.
First, they are inconsistent with the results of other surveys using the

Table 4.3 Spousal Violence Surveys: Canada, 1981-1994

Author(s)	Survey	Place	Size	Composition	Conflict Tactics Scale	Feminist	Criminal Code	Total Violence Past Year		Severe Violence		Violence Ever		Homicide	
		Sample			Measures			Findings (Victims of Violence)							
								Men	Women	Men	Women	Men	Women	Men	Women
Brinkerhoff & Lupri (1988)	1981	Calgary	562	Couples aged 18 years and over	x	—	—	13.3	10.3	10.7	4.8	—	—	—	—
Smith (1985)	1985	Toronto	315	Women aged 18 to 25 years	x	—	—	—	10.8	—	—	—	18.1	—	—
Lupri	1986	Canada	1,530	Men and women, ever married or cohabiting	x	—	—	—	17.8	—	10.1	—	—	—	—
Kennedy & Dulton (1987)	1986	Alberta	1,045	Adult men & women (18 years and over)	x	—	—	—	11.2	—	2.3	—	—	—	—
Smith (1987)	1987	Toronto	604	Adult women formerly or presently married, cohabiting, or dating	x	—	—	—	14.4	—	5.1	—	36.4	—	—
Somer et. al.	1992	Winnipeg	452	Adult females presently married or cohabiting (aged 18-65 years)	x	—	—	39.1	—	—	—	—	—	—	—

Study	Year	Location	N	Sample											
Somer	1994	Winnipeg	452	Adult females presently married or cohabiting (aged 18-65 years)	—	—	39.1	26.3	—	—	—	—	—	—	—
Statistics Canada (1993)	1993	Canada	12,300	Adult females aged 18 years and over	x	—	—	3.0	—	—	—	—	29.0	—	—
Wilson and Daly (1994)	1994	Canada	1886	Males and females married, separated or divorced	—	x	—	—	—	—	—	—	—	30.0	70.0
Lupri, Grandin, and Brinkerhoff (1994)	1987	Canada	435	Adult males, ever married or cohabiting	—	—	—	35.9	—	9.9	—	—	—	—	—
Ellis (1994)	1990	Hamilton	247	Adult males, females, and couples who were separating	x	x	36.7	56.7	—	—	22.0	41.5	—	—	—
Ellis (1994)	1990	Hamilton	247	Adult males, females, and couples who were separating	x	x	—	—	13.1	21.7	28.0	29.9	—	—	—

41

same instrument (CTS), similar samples, and covering the same time span (12 months). Thus, in addition to results reported by Brinkerhoff and Lupri (1988), Straus (1989) found that U.S. wives were sole perpetrators of conflict-instigated violence in 25.5% of the cases and husbands were sole perpetrators in 25.9% of the cases. Using the CTS but covering a different time period and sample, Ellis (1994) also found symmetry in conflict-instigated spousal violence. Last, Lupri's findings contradict those of Somer. In Lupri's Calgary study, 13.3% of male partners reported being the victims of conflict-instigated spousal violence. However, the results of his national study indicate that 17.8% of female partners reported being the victims of this form of spousal violence.

Males are more likely than female partners to engage in control-instigated violence, but Somer (1994) and Somer et al. (1992) ignored this type of violence. The Somer et al. explanation of female partner violence leads to the conclusion that male partners are far more likely than female partners to behave violently toward their partners.

This last point needs elaboration. According to Somer et al. (1992), "females with male personality traits" (p. 1321) are greatly overrepresented among females who were violent toward their male partners. If, as they state, malelike female partners are much more likely than other female partners to behave violently toward their partners, is it not logical to conclude that male partners are much more likely than female and female-like female partners to abuse their partners psychologically and physically?

Using the same measure (CTS) as did Lupri (1990), Ellis (1994) found female partners were more likely than male partners to report being the victims of severe conflict-instigated violence (21.7% vs. 13.1%). This finding, based on a sample of couples whose answers were cross-checked, contradicts the Lupri (Calgary) findings on the gender patterning of severe, conflict-instigated spousal violence.

When both the CTS and feminist measures are used, the former reveals gender symmetry in spousal violence, the latter, gender asymmetry. More specifically, compared with males, a far higher proportion of female partners reported being the victims of control-instigated violence during the preceding year (56.7% vs. 36.7%) and ever (41.5% vs. 22.0%). Approximately equal proportions of male and female partners reported being the victims of conflict-instigated violence during these two time periods: 21.1% versus 13.1% and 29.9% versus 28.0%, respectively (Ellis, 1994). Tables 4.4 and 4.5 provide more detailed findings on gender differences in control-instigated and conflict-instigated spousal violence.

The spouses whose reports of conflict-instigated violence are presented in Table 4.4 are couples. The Spousal Sex Ratio of Assailants (SSROA) 1 and 2 are measures of gender differences in abusing and being abused by spouses. More specifically, the SSROA measures the ratio of wives to husbands who admit abusing their partners (admitters, SSROA-1) and the ratio of wives to husbands who are accused by their partners of abusing them (accused, SSROA-2). Table 4.4 presents these two ratios for each of the CTS items listed and also for all five combined.

For all five items, the SSROA-1 (admitted assailants) is 99. This means that for every 100 husbands who admitted abusing their wives in one or more of the five ways listed, 99 wives admitted doing the same thing. SSROA-1, in short, is approximately equal; gender symmetry prevails. Across different CTS items, gender differences in ratios range from 22 (hitting) to 80 (slapping). Hitting is the most serious form of abuse included in Table 4.4. Here, 22 husbands admit hitting their wives for every 100 wives who admit hitting their husbands. However, an SSROA-2 of 94 indicates that an approximately equal number of wives and husbands are accused by their partners of hitting them: For every 100 husbands who accuse their wives of hitting them, 94 wives accuse their husbands of the same thing. Among accused assailants, gender differences in ratios vary from 62 (slapping) to 96 (threatening). For all five items (total), the SSROA-1 (admitted assailants) is 99 and the SSROA-2 (accused assailants) is 96. This means that for every 100 wives who admit abusing their husbands, 99 husbands admit abusing their wives, and for every 100 wives accused by their husbands of abusing them in one or more of the five ways listed, 96 husbands are accused by their wives of doing the same thing. Gender symmetry in conflict-instigated marital violence clearly prevails among ex-partners.

In addition to the CTS, violence between separating couples was measured by a number of questions included in the questionnaires administered to clients in the lawyer and mediator samples. Findings presented in Table 4.5 reveal that a markedly higher proportion of wives

Table 4.4 The Spousal Sex Ratio of Assailants (SSROA) Among Separating Couples

CTS Items[c]	Assailants: Admitted[a]			Assailants: Accused[b]		
	Wives	Husbands	SSROA-1[d]	Wives	Husbands	SSROA-2
Threatened to hit or throw something	16	12	75	24	23	96
Threw, smashed, or hit something	18	27	67	36	28	76
Pushed, grabbed, or shoved	19	24	79	32	28	88
Slapped	10	8	80	13	21	62
Hit with something	9	2	22	16	17	94
Total	72	73	99	122	117	96

NOTE: $N = 59$.

a. Partner admits (reports) abusing his or her partner in the manner indicated by the CTS item.

b. Partner accuses partner of abusing him or her in the manner indicated by the CTS item.

c. The remaining three CTS (indicating severe violence) items (choked, threatened to use gun or knife, and used gun or knife) were not included because only 3 spouses either admitted doing one or more of these things or were accused of them by their partners.

d. The SSROA-1 is calculated by dividing the longer number of assailants into the smaller and multiplying by 100. Thus, $12/16 \times 100 = 75$ for the "threatened to hit" item. This means that for every 100 wives who admitted doing this, 75 husbands made the same admission. For the next CTS item (threw, smashed, or hit), the ratio is reversed. Here, SSROA-1 = 67 means that for every 100 husbands who admitted throwing and so on, only 67 wives admitted to engaging in the same conduct. Totals do not sum to 59 because partners may engage in more than one violent act.

in the two samples reported being abused by their partners. Specifically, almost two thirds of the wives (61.0%) and less than one third of the husbands (31.4%) reported partner's physical or emotional abuse as a major reason for separating, 56.7% of wives and 36.7% of husbands reported being physically, emotionally, or verbally hurt by their ex-partners during the last 6 months they were together, and almost twice the number of wives reported being physically hurt intentionally by their ex-husbands (41.5% vs. 22.0%) at some time during their marriage.

The spousal sex ratio of the three violence items included in Table 4.5 was also calculated. For every 23 husbands who reported physical or emotional abuse as a major reason for separating, 100 wives did so.

Table 4.5 Control-Instigated Abuse Reported by Wives and Husbands, Total Sample (by percentage)

Questions	Wives (n = 247)	Husbands (n = 112)
Was your partner's physical or emotional abuse a major reason for separating?	61.0	31.4**
Did you experience physical, emotional, or verbal abuse by your ex-partner for any reason not connected with an ongoing conflict during the 6 months before you separated?	56.7	36.7**
Did your ex-partner physically hurt you intentionally, for any reason, ever?	41.5	22.0*

$*p<.01; **p<.001.$

For every 29 husbands who reported experiencing physical or emotional hurting for any reason not connected with an ongoing conflict during the 6 months before separation, 100 wives did so. For every 23 husbands who reported being physically hurt intentionally, ever, by their ex-partner, 100 wives did so.

Taken together, the findings presented in Tables 4.4 and 4.5 indicate that gender asymmetry characterizes the pattern of control-instigated violence between separating couples, with separating wives reporting higher rates of victimization than separating husbands.

In sum, the preceding analysis of the evidence presented provides support for the following:

Summary of Findings

Female partners who were married to generally aggressive males, and especially a small subset of them classified as sociopathic batterers, are most likely to be seriously injured by them following marital separation or divorce.

Physical or psychological abuse as a major reason for separating is cited by 61% of female partners and 31% of male partners.

Husbands are far more likely to kill wives than wives are to kill husbands.

Compared with female partners, a significantly higher proportion of male partners engage in control-instigated violence.

Approximately equal proportions of male and female partners engage in conflict-instigated violence.

Conclusion

▓ Because of the invariable copresence of two types of spousal violence—violence as a tactic of conflict settlement and violence as a means of control—the incidence prevalence and gender patterning of spousal violence should be measured by administering both the CTS and questions addressing violence as control.

Notes

1. For a more detailed description of these two approaches, see Dobash and Dobash (1992) and Ellis and Wight (1995). See also Haynes (1992).

2. In responding to criticisms raised by Roberts (1992), mediators such as Haynes (1992) and Blume (1993) point out that contemporary family system approaches place less emphasis on the causal power attributed to the family as a closed system. History, wider societal influences, and individual variations among family members are also recognized as being partly responsible for spousal, parental, and sibling behavior. Blume (1992) also notes that "relatively few authors have specified how their approaches are informed by [family-systems-based theoretical] ideas" (p. 197). In addition to Roberts (1992), Bograd (1984); Enns (1988); Grillo (1991); and Libow, Raskin, and Caust (1982) have criticized the application of family systems theory in mediation and counseling.

3. Also see Bograd (1988), Hamner and Maynard (1987), Jones (1994), Martin (1976), Radford (1992), and Schechter (1982).

4. For a discussion of the compatibility between mediation and feminism, see Rifkin (1984).

5. See also Domestic Abuse Intervention Project (1984), Edwards (1987), and Stanko (1987). Kelly (1987) defines male violence as a continuum in which violence is "connected to more common, everyday aspects of male behavior . . . [where] 'typical' and 'aberrant' male behavior shade into one another" (pp. 50-51).

6. For a more detailed discussion of theory and research on instrumental and expressive violence in a variety of social settings, see Ellis and Wight (1995).

7. For example, based on their research on high-conflict families, Johnston and Campbell (1993) offer an inductive definition of violence that links conflict and control-instigated

violence: "At the interactional level, violence is a way to regain or maintain interpersonal control in the event of a conflict of interest between family members" (p. 191).

8. This ratio is reported for Chicago, not the United States as a whole. In Chicago and elsewhere, the spousal sex ratio of killing varies with marital status. Compared with registered unions, common-law couples and cohabitants have higher homicide rates. Among African Americans in Chicago, the spousal sex ratio of killings favoring female killers is higher among common-law and cohabiting couples. For a more detailed discussion, see Dobash et al. (1992), Ellis (1994), Mercy and Saltzman (1989), and Wilson and Daly (1994).

9. See Dobash et al. (1992), Ellis and DeKeseredy (1995), and Wilson and Daly (1994).

Spousal Violence
Postseparation

A number of scholars and activists have drawn attention to the positive association between estrangement or separation and violence toward women. Thus, as Pagelow (1993) contends, "Risks of extreme violence, rape and homicide are highest when [wives] seek freedom" (p. 69). Wilson and Daly (1994) present findings indicating that separated wives are six times more likely to be killed by their ex-husbands than coresiding wives are by their husbands (p. 8).[1] Wife abuse surveys reveal that separated or divorced women reported the highest rates of wife abuse (Ellis & DeKeseredy, 1989; Kennedy & Dutton, 1989; Lupri, 1990; Strauss & Gelles, 1990).[2]

This body of evidence may convey the impression that all separating or separated women are equally likely to be murdered, assaulted, or psychologically abused by their ex-partners. Research evidence indicates that this is not true. During the years 1974 to 1992, one in 21,739 separated women was killed by her ex-husband (Wilson & Daly, 1994). Clearly, and tragically, some separated women were killed, but the vast majority were not. Again, approximately one third of the separated or divorced women in Smith's (1990) sample reported being abused by their partners, but more than two thirds did not.

A number of factors may help explain why some separated or divorced women are killed, beaten, or psychologically abused by their ex-partners, whereas others are not. One of these may be the type of legal separation process they participated in. Lawyer negotiations is one such process, a process used by 80% to 90% of separating couples, and mediation is the other.[3]

Critics of mediation assert that a disproportionately high number of female victims of repeated violence by male partners and ex-partners are found among those participating in the process of mediation. We shall present two lines of evidence that address this assertion. First, research evidence on the effect of mediation on violence toward coresiding female partners will be reviewed. Then we shall review evidence comparing the effects of mediation and lawyer negotiations on violence between separated couples.

One of the earliest and most influential critics of mediation was lawyer Lisa Lerman. In 1984, she wrote an article criticizing the diversion of wife abuse cases from "formal legal action combined with punishment or rehabilitation" to mediation (Lerman, 1984, p. 70). In her view, the law enforcement model is more effective in ensuring the safety of abused women.[4] Among the mechanisms underlying its greater effectiveness are the law's focus on stopping the violence; compelling the abuser to accept personal responsibility for his violent, criminal behavior; and fostering community responsibility for stopping the violence.

In support of the hypothesis that the law enforcement model is more effective than mediation in stopping the violence, Lerman cites the research of Bethel and Singer (1982; mediation process) and Sherman and Berk (1989; law enforcement model).

In 1982, Bethel and Singer published the results of their evaluation of the District of Columbia Mediation Service, Washington, D.C. This service was provided under the auspices of the District of Columbia Citizen Complaint Center. Victims of domestic violence who filed complaints were provided with the option of having their cases mediated if they both agreed and were both still involved in an ongoing relationship. Cases were screened out if the injuries were serious, a gun was used to threaten the victim, or the violence was repetitive.

Two months after mediation agreement was reached, mediation staff conducted telephone interviews with each of the participants. The terms of the mediated agreements included stopping the violence. Telephone interview data revealed that 93% of the partners whose violence had instigated a complaint reported complying with the terms of the agreement. A smaller but still relatively high percentage of complainants (73%) also reported that their abusers were complying with the agreements 2 months after they had signed them. If complainants' reports of respondents' abusive behavior are treated as the most reliable evidence on postmediation abuse, then we find that 4 of 51 respondents (8%) abused their partners and another 4 (8%) harassed theirs. This means that 16% of the respondents in the sample assaulted or harassed their partners at some time during the 2 months following the mediation of their domestic violence complaint and 84% did not.

Lerman does not cite these findings. Instead, she confines her criticism to the screening criteria used by Bethel and Singer. She does cite the findings of Sherman and Berk (1989) and implies that arresting wife abusers is more effective in stopping wife abuse. A number of methodological differences, however, including different measures of violence (criminal and noncriminal vs. criminal only) and different postintervention observation periods (2 months vs. 6 months) make it hazardous to draw conclusions on the basis of a comparison of the two sets of findings.

At the time the Sherman and Berk study was conducted (1981-1982), arresting wife abusers was so rare as to constitute a formal legal alternative to the use of such informal dispute resolution processes as separating the abusers and victims or mediating their disputes. In their experimental field study, Sherman and Berk (1989) compared the effects of arresting, separating, and mediating 314 offender-present cases of misdemeanant (relatively minor) assaults on female partners by the same male partner on the same victim 6 months later. They found the repeat assault rates officially recorded by police for the arrested, separated, and mediated groups were 10%, 24%, and 17%, respectively. The difference between the arrest and separated groups was statistically significant ($p < .05$) but the difference between the arrest and mediated groups was not. Thus, these findings provide qualified support for the law enforcement model: A formal legal sanction (arrest) is more effective than separation but no more effective than mediation in reducing misdemeanant repeat assaults on female partners.

It is relevant to note that the mediation treatment as delivered by the police officers who participated in the study was defined for them as "a means of getting to the underlying cause of the dispute (in which both partners are implicitly assumed to be at fault)" (Lerman, 1984, p. 263). The officers were not trained mediators, and the parties involved participated in only one so-called mediation session. Still, even this weak version of mediation was as effective as the strong formal legal sanction of arrest in reducing repeat assaults. The findings of the Sherman and Berk study, then, cannot be cited as a basis for concluding that the law enforcement model is more effective than mediation in reducing repeat assaults of wives.

The Sherman and Berk study—a fine achievement at the time—was characterized by a number of methodological problems.[5] Two subsequent experimental field studies successfully avoided many of them. The two best designed and conducted studies to date are the replications in Omaha, Nebraska, and Charlotte, North Carolina, of Sherman and Berk's Minneapolis study.

Dunford, Huisinga, and Elliott (1990) delivered the same three treatments—arrest, separate, mediate—to 330 offender-present cases in Omaha. They found that the "at least one repeat arrest for assault rate" for the arrested, separated, and mediated groups was 11.0%, 11.3%, and 8.7%, respectively. Victim interviews revealed that at least one injury was reported by 14.7% of the arrested cases and 20.4% of the cases not arrested.[6] The differences are not statistically significant. On the basis of these findings, the authors concluded that "victims whose partners were arrested were no less likely to experience repeat violence from that partner than were victims whose partners received a randomized separate or mediate treatment" (p. 196).

The Charlotte findings by Hirschel, Hutchinson, and Dean (1992) are similar to those reported for Omaha. The sample consisted of 686 cases. During the 6-month posttreatment period, at least one arrest for an assault was reported for 18.2% of arrest treatment cases, 11.8% for the mediated cases, and 19.2% for the citation (summons) cases.[7] These findings suggest that arresting assailants actually increased the likelihood of repeat assaults. Taken together, criminalizing the incident (arresting and giving a citation) increased the risk of repeat assaults by a ratio of 1.6 to 1 (Sherman, 1992).

Hirschel et al. (1992) point out that "the differences which do exist between these treatments are . . . not substantially significant. These findings in no way would justify police moving to an informal response to spouse assault as the preferred action" (p. 113). However, if 70 more women were assaulted following an arrest or citation than was the case following an informal police response (separate or mediate), surely this is of substantive significance to them (Sherman, 1992)!

Additional support for the hypothesis that arrest increases wife assault is provided by data from the Omaha study. Thus, 1 year following arrest, suspect assailants in the arrest group had a higher number of new arrests than did suspect assailants in the separate and mediate groups. These differences are statistically significant (Sherman, 1992).[8]

Some time after the Sherman and Berk study had been published, Sherman reports that Berk told him about a finding that had not been published: Most of the victims who had been interviewed reported that their relationships had broken up following the arrival of the police. Thus, one noteworthy policing effect was separation for a majority of partners in the arrest, separate, and mediate groups (Sherman, 1992). Because these couples were not followed, we do not know what happened to them. Most may have simply split up. Some may have had their separations negotiated by lawyers, and a few may have participated in family mediation. Had this occurred, would females in the latter group have experienced higher rates of postprocessing violence than members of the former group?

Mediation and Adversarial Process Effects

In 1990, Kelly (1990b) published a longitudinal study of the effects of adversarial and mediated divorce cases on a number of outcomes during the processing of cases and at three points in time after processing had been completed. Violence between partners was not a measured outcome, but two of its correlates, anger and conflict, were.

One of Kelly's (1990b) major hypotheses was that "divorce mediation . . . would lead to fewer and less intense conflicts in the two years after divorce" (p. 12). Controlling for the presence of young children and frequency of ex-partner contact, she found no statistical differences in the frequency of overall conflict between partners in the mediated and adversarial groups.

When the frequency and intensity of conflict were measured at earlier periods of time, the first part of Kelly's hypothesis was confirmed. She found that partners in the mediation group reported significantly less conflict over a range of specific issues (e.g., child rearing, children's education, custody, access, child support) than did partners in the adversarial group.

Statistically significant predictors of conflict between ex-partners 2 years after divorce were (a) the presence of young children 1 year after divorce and (b) the level of conflict when divorce processing started. The type of intervention (adversarial vs. mediation) was included in the regression model being tested, but as indicated earlier, it was found not to be a statistically significant predictor of postprocessing conflict.

Among male partners, only High Anger (a composite variable made up of high anger at spouse, perceived high anger of ex-spouse at self, and high negative feelings toward ex-spouse) was found to be a statistically significant predictor of high levels of conflict 2 years after the divorce. There were five (or more) variables in the model being tested, and High Anger alone accounted for 36% of the total variance in the level of conflict.

Among female partners, High Anger, presence of young children, and noncompliance with support payment arrangements were found to be statistically significant predictors of the level of conflict 2 years after divorce. For both males and females, the type of intervention was included in the model being tested but was not found to be a statistically significant predictor.

On the basis of these findings, we may conclude that the effect of intervention (adversarial vs. mediation) on the frequency and intensity of partner conflict varies over time. During divorce processing and 1 year after processing has been completed, the partner-controlled process of mediation is more effective that the lawyer-controlled adversarial process in reducing the frequency and intensity of conflicts. Two years after divorce, differences in the amount and level of conflict reported by ex-partners in the mediated and adversarial groups become insignificant. Male and female partners who were very angry at the start of divorce processing were more likely to report high and highly intense levels of conflict 2 years after divorce, regardless of their membership in the mediated or adversarial groups.

If it is reasonable to assume that conflicts instigated by anger are strongly associated with violence (physical, verbal, emotional), then we may interpret Kelly's (1990b) findings as demonstrating (albeit indirectly) the effects of mediation and the adversarial process on postprocessing violence among divorcing and divorced ex-partners.

A more direct test of the effect of one of these two processes on postprocessing violence among separated women was conducted by Ellis and Stuckless (1992). In this study, two mediation samples (voluntary vs. coerced) were selected. The voluntary sample included clients ($n = 41$) participating in publicly funded mediation offered by a court-based mediation service. On the average, these clients who voluntarily chose to have their separations mediated attended six 1-hour mediation sessions.

The coerced sample consisted of 32 clients who were participating in mediation offered by Legal Aid. They actually participated in only one mediation session. Their participation was coerced because it was instigated by the threat of withdrawing their publicly funded family certificate. This would mean they would have to pay the lawyers who represented them.

One of the major findings of this study was that the partners participating in single coerced mediation sessions were more likely than partners voluntarily participating in a number of court-based mediation sessions to report higher levels of physical and verbal aggression by their partners after the mediation process was completed.

Legal Aid clients were represented by Legal Aid lawyers prior to the termination of the process by a mediation session. Processing by lawyer negotiations invariably involved the completion of an affidavit by both parties. These affidavits included content that was hurtful and damaging to the parties. Completing an affidavit was a statistically significant predictor of calls to the police by female ex-partners following mediation.

In this study, the effect of "hassles" prior to mediation were also examined. Hassles were measured by questions about such things as being "bothered . . . , prevented from leaving home, car, workplace" and "having personal property damaged" (Ellis & Stuckless, 1992, p. 214). For example, as a whole ($n = 37$), premediation hassles—more validly conceived of as harassment or stalking—were found to be a statistically significant predictor of postmediation violence toward females by their male ex-partners.

The Ellis and Stuckless (1992) study compared the effects of participation in two types of mediation on postprocessing violence between

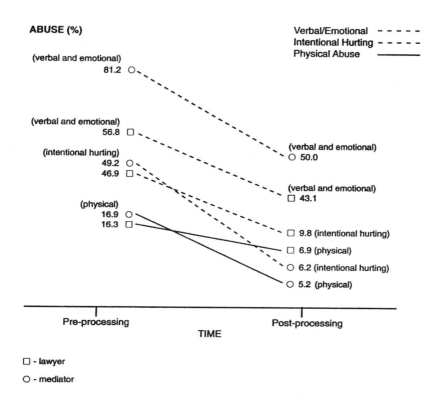

Figure 5.1. Pre- and Post-Processing Spousal Abuse of Female Partners in the Mediation and Lawyer Samples

separated partners. The Family Mediation Pilot Study (Ellis, 1994) compares the relative effects of publicly funded court-based mediation and publicly funded lawyer negotiations on the same outcome.

Figure 5.1 shows changes in the proportion of females in the mediation and lawyer client samples reporting nonconflict-related abuse before and after the processing of their separations.

An examination of this figure yields the following findings. First, all three forms of abuse (emotional, verbal, physical) decreased following processing. Second, some forms of violence decreased more markedly than others. Thus, clients of lawyers reported a 37.1% decrease in intentional hurting (from 46.9% to 9.8%) and only a 13.7% decrease in verbal and emotional abuse (from 56.8% to 43.1%). Among clients of mediators, intentional hurting decreased by 43.0% (from 49.2% to 6.2%), whereas verbal and emotional abuse decreased from 81.2% to 50.0%, a decrease of 31.2%.

Third, when the four types of abuse were included in a composite measure (Abuse Scale), we found a statistically significant difference in the proportion of mediation and lawyer clients reporting preprocessing abuse. Specifically, a significantly higher proportion of mediation clients reported being abused. Differences in postprocessing abuse, however, were not statistically significant.

Fourth, the greatest reported decreases in abuse were reported for verbal and emotional abuse by mediation clients.

Fifth, after the processing of their separations had been completed, approximately 6% of females in both samples reported being physically abused, and about 8% reported being intentionally hurt by their ex-partners.

Females in the mediation and lawyer samples also reported on the conflict-instigated abuse they experienced before and after the legal processing of their separations (using the CTS). Decreases in "minor" and "serious" physical abuse were not statistically significant. The mean or average number of serious abuse incidents was higher for females in the lawyer sample. Because the numbers involved are small, however, this finding must be accepted with some caution. At the same time, it is consistent with the findings for emotional and verbal abuse.

In interpreting the findings, two considerations are relevant. First, the single most important factor responsible for the decreases in post-processing abuse presented in Figure 5.1 is the fact of separation. Physical separation decreases physical abuse by decreasing the opportunities for both conflict-instigated and control-instigated abuse.

Second, female mediation clients reported higher preprocessing levels of abuse on the physical, verbal, and emotional abuse scale. This difference was statistically significant ($p < .05$). Postprocessing differences in abuse scale scores reported by female clients in the two samples were not significantly different. These findings indicate that mediators started the process with a higher proportion of abused female clients than lawyers did. However, by the end of the mediation process, the proportion of female clients reporting postprocessing abuse in the two samples was approximately the same. This suggests that mediation, far from increasing postprocessing abuse, actually made a contribution toward decreasing it.

Another source of support for this interpretation comes from comparing the mean or average levels of serious conflict-instigated abuse for female mediation and lawyer clients before mediation and lawyer negotiation started and after they were completed. The preprocessing means scores were approximately equal; postprocessing mean scores, however, were higher for lawyer than for mediation clients. Actually, the difference was almost statistically significant ($p<.07$). In short, female lawyer and mediation clients began the legal processing of their separations as equals with respect to the amount of serious conflict-instigated abuse their partners had directed toward them, but 12 months after their separations had been processed, female lawyer clients reported a higher amount of the same kind of abuse by their ex-partners.

Incidents of postprocessing abuse reported by female lawyer clients were not confined to conflict-instigated abuse. In fact, quantitative and qualitative data indicate that control-instigated abuse was more likely to occur. A female client whose ex-partner wanted more frequent access to their children reported that "he came to my apartment. He kicked and punched me, pushed me into a closet and started screaming. He went home, called the police and tried to lay an assault charge against me" (Ellis, 1994, p. 42).

During their marriage, the same woman reported "ongoing verbal abuse, manipulation and physical threats." She reported that relations with her ex-partner became worse since the processing of her separation and that she and her children were afraid of his "assaults, manipulation and [attempts] to take away the children" (Ellis, 1994, p. 44).

Another female lawyer client reported that after completing the legal processing of their separation, her "normally calm and controlled" ex-partner "verbally abused and punched me. It still hurts to this day" (Ellis, 1994, p. 46).

More ominously, a third female lawyer client first reported that "mediation is critically important because of extensive social problems," and then makes the following observation:

Legal process invites ongoing conflict [after completion of the separation process]. Safety of the ex-spouses, particularly the women, is becoming

more critical as men seem to feel that to end harassment [legal wrangling],
it would be more beneficial to kill ex-spouse and serve sentence of 2 years
or less, be given custody of children, . . . and be free of hassle. (Ellis, 1994,
p. 46)

Compared with lawyer negotiations, then, mediation was found to
make a greater contribution toward reducing postprocessing abuse.

But, one may object, is it not possible or even likely that factors other
than mediation or lawyer negotiations really account for these findings?
For example, a higher proportion of female clients in the lawyer or
mediation samples may have been (a) physically or nonphysically abused
or both prior to the processing of their separations, (b) more recently
abused (i.e., abused during the 6 months prior to separating), (c)
separated for a longer period of time prior to the processing of their
separation (time being a healer of wounds), (d) living with abusive
partners who also had drug or alcohol problems, or (e) poorly educated
or poorer economically or both (these are correlated with wife abuse;
Smith, 1987).

Hypotheses involving these five rival explanatory factors were formulated and tested. Four of them were not confirmed. That is to say,
the differences between the female mediation and lawyer client samples
with respect to factors a, c, d, and e were not statistically significant. In
addition, the association between each of these factors and postprocessing physical abuse and intentional hurting was not statistically significant. On the basis of these findings, we conclude that they do not
account for the findings described earlier.

There is a statistically significant difference between females in the
two samples with respect to the recency of abuse (factor b). More
specifically, a significantly higher proportion of females in the lawyer
sample (67.0% vs. 46.2%) reported being abused during the 6 months
prior to separating ($p < .05$). Moreover, recency of abuse is significantly
associated with the choice of lawyer negotiations ($p < .05$) and with the
postprocessing verbal abuse ($p < .05$). The association between recency
of abuse and physical abuse, intentionally hurting, and verbal abuse is
not statistically significant. On the basis of these findings, we conclude
that recency of abuse does not account for differences in the before-after
and after-before abuse patterns for female lawyer and mediation clients.

Having eliminated a number of rival or alternative explanations, we
turned our attention to the problem of identifying mechanisms that

would explain why the patterns for intentional hurting and physical abuse reported by female mediation and lawyer clients are different. Previous research (Ellis & Stuckless, 1992) suggested that completing an affidavit may be implicated in these outcomes. The postprocessing questionnaire included six affidavit-related questions. Of these, one was especially significant. This was, "Did your affidavit contain true statements or information that would hurt your partner?"

The next step involved examining the association between completing an affidavit with hurtful content and postprocessing abuse. The association was statistically significant ($p<.05$). This finding supports the conclusion that completing an affidavit with hurtful content is one of the mechanisms accounting for the statistically significant differences in the before-after and after-before patterns reported by female lawyer and mediation clients.

Qualitative data gathered by Ellis (1994) provided further support for this conclusion. Representative comments from lawyer clients read as follows: "[There is] too much emphasis on affidavits" (male; p. 61) and "Mediation would be a good alternative to reduce stress and conflict frequently caused by affidavits" (female; p. 60).

In this connection, it is relevant to note that we may have underestimated the negative effect of this factor by asking about the inclusion of true hurtful content rather than *any* (true or untrue) hurtful content in affidavits. If hurtful but true statements increase the likelihood of postprocessing physical abuse, untrue hurtful statements may be associated with even greater increases in the probability of physical abuse following the processing of separations.

On the other hand, the comparison between a mediation pilot project and lawyer negotiations may have increased the positive (physical abuse preventive) effect of the former relative to the latter. In the Ellis (1994) comparison and evaluation study, lawyer negotiations were compared with a court-based mediation process that was changed in a number of ways. These changes were in place during the 3-year study period. Included among them were changes facilitating the disclosure of partner abuse from the first to the last mediation session. These changes, and their consistent implementation by staff mediators, probably make the pilot mediation process we studied unique or at least unusual. Taken together, they may have contributed to narrowing postprocessing differences in partner abuse between mediation and lawyer clients by bringing about greater decreases in abuse among clients of mediators.

Predictors of Postseparation Abuse

The penultimate step in accounting for postprocessing abuse involved an examination of the associations among all of the variables referred to earlier, including those that are possible rival or alternative explanatory factors. Perusal of two correlation matrices for the mediation and lawyer samples (Ellis, 1994) reveals that the association between pre-processing and postprocessing abuse is statistically significant among lawyer clients ($p < .01$) but not among mediation clients. On the other hand, the association between partner's drug or alcohol problems and postprocessing abuse is statistically significant among mediation clients ($p < .05$) but not among lawyer clients. The association between monthly income and postprocessing abuse is not statistically significant among clients in either sample. The association between level of education and postprocessing abuse is statistically significant among lawyer clients ($p < .01$) but not among mediation clients.

The association between recency of abuse and postprocessing abuse is statistically significant in the lawyer sample ($p < .05$) but not in the mediation sample. Length of separation and postprocessing abuse are not significantly associated in either the mediation or the lawyer sample.

Taken together, correlational data revealed that 9 of the 18 variables are significantly associated with postprocessing abuse. The last step in the analysis involved entering 6 variables suggested by prior research and theory into a model that revealed how well they accounted for postprocessing abuse, individually (when the effects of the other variables were controlled) and jointly. Regression analysis (ordinary least squares) did this. The results of regressing postprocessing abuse (scale) on these seven variables are presented in Ellis (1994).

In the Ellis (1994) report, seven variables jointly explain 38% of the total variance. This is a very respectable figure. Moreover, the model itself is statistically significant ($F < .01$). Three of the six variables are statistically significant predictors of postprocessing abuse. These are (a) completing an affidavit with hurtful content, (b) level of education, and (c) recency of abuse. Of these three variables, completing an affidavit with hurtful content accounts for most (14.0%) of the total variation explained (i.e., 38.0%).

These results as well as the results of the other stepwise regression analyses in which choice of mediator or lawyer negotiations was entered as a predictor variable indicate that the mechanism that prevented the achievement of greater decreases in postprocessing abuse among female lawyer clients was the inclusion of hurtful content in affidavits.

In addition to this lawyer-influenced mechanism, nonsignificant decreases in postprocessing physical abuse among lawyer clients were also predicted by two factors over which lawyers have little control. These are (a) the level of education of their clients—they are more poorly educated than mediation clients—and (b) recency of abuse—more lawyer than mediation clients reported being recently abused.

Summary of Findings

Repeat wife-assault rates varied with the type of police intervention, the rates being higher for arrested assailants than for assailants whose cases were mediated.

At 2 years postdivorce, there were no differences in the frequency and intensity of conflicts between ex-partners who participated in mediation or the adversarial process.

Postprocessing rates of wife abuse varied with participation in multisession voluntary or single-session coerced mediation, with the rates being higher in the latter.

Postprocessing rates of male violence toward female ex-partners in the mediation and lawyer client groups decreased following separation, with greater decreases being reported by ex-partners in the mediation sample.

High initial (preprocessing) levels of anger, presence of young children, and noncompliance with child support arrangements were better predictors of the frequency and intensity of ex-partner conflicts than either mediation or lawyer negotiation.

Conclusions

▓ Separation markedly decreases the likelihood of nonlethal postprocessing violence.

▓ The passage of time (2 years) is more effective than either mediation or lawyer negotiations in reducing the frequency and intensity of conflicts between ex-partners.

- ▨ Voluntary mediation makes a greater contribution to preventing postprocessing violence toward female ex-partners than does coerced mediation.

- ▨ Voluntary mediation makes a greater contribution toward preventing postprocessing violence toward female ex-partners than does lawyer negotiation.

- ▨ The greater effectiveness of mediation over lawyer negotiation in preventing postprocessing conflicts is restricted to conflicts occurring within 12 months of participating in these two dispute resolution processes.

- ▨ One factor underlying the relative ineffectiveness of lawyer negotiation in preventing postprocessing violence toward female partners is the completion of affidavits with hurtful content.

Notes

1. See also Easteal (1993); Fischer, Vidmar, & Ellis (1993); Jones (1994); and Mahoney (1991).

2. The time ordering of abuse (before or after separation or both) is not clear in these surveys. Findings presented later in this chapter indicate that a far higher proportion of the abuse reported in the wife abuse surveys occurred prior to separation, when the opportunity for husbands to abuse their wives was much greater.

3. This estimate is based on a random sample of divorce and separation files at the Hamilton United Family Court and the Hull, Quebec, Family Court. A number of couples simply separate without involving legal processing in the courts. We do not know who they are or what proportion of separations they account for.

4. For a more recent statement of support for the law enforcement model over mediation, see Cobb (1992). For an attempt to integrate the law enforcement model and family mediation see Attorney General (1989).

5. Sherman (1992) has done a good job of discussing these problems. Several contributors to the *American Behavioral Scientist* (1994) have also discussed the methodological strengths and weaknesses of the Sherman and Berk study as well as the six replication studies. For another detailed evaluation of these studies, see the whole issue of *Journal of Criminal Law and Criminology* (1992).

6. Because arrested abusers spent varying amounts of time in jail, the opportunity for them to hit or hurt their partners was reduced in comparison with those whose cases were mediated. Differential opportunity could help explain some of the differences between the arrest and nonarrest cases.

7. In interpreting these findings, it is important to note that only 47% of the sample completed the 6-month interview.

8. Findings from the Omaha and Minneapolis studies indicate that the escalation-of-violence effect of arrest varies with the employment status of the assailant, with higher postarrest rates of assault being reported for unemployed males. Employed males were more likely to be deterred by arrest.

Power Imbalances in Divorce Mediation

Gender and power figure prominently in feminist critiques of mediation.[1] In them, structural inequality favoring males is (correctly) taken for granted. Not only do males occupy dominant positions in most major institutions (e.g., military, business, political, familial, religious, educational, legal), but male dominance is also normatively legitimated. Gender inequality and a supporting ideology are essential elements in what Dobash and Dobash (1979) refer to as the *patriarchy*. In patriarchal societies, systemic gender inequality is associated with differences in social power. Males as a gender group have significantly more power than females as a gender group.[2]

Having correctly assumed the existence of gender inequality and systemic power differences at the level of society, some feminists go on to assume that these differences also characterize individual male and female partners who are in the process of separating or divorcing. Anne Bottomley (1984), an informed, articulate feminist, offers a not unrepresentative critique. According to her, "Women's needs, the consequences of their continuing position of disadvantage in society, their lack of bargaining power vis-à-vis individual men . . . make them particularly vulnerable in conciliation [mediation] procedures" (p. 298). Bottomley goes on to contend that mediators who "ignore the structural conflicts between the interests and needs of women and men . . . reproduce existing power relationships" (p. 297). Here, mediators are constructed as agents of patriarchy because the professional norm of neutrality requires them to ignore gender inequality.

Like their critics, many mediators and their supporters take the existence of systemic gender inequality as given and regard gendered power differences as "central to the mediation process" (Neumann, 1992, p. 228). Unlike their critics, however, mediators contend that spousal power differences that exist at the level of society may not be present, or present but not to the same degree, among individual male and female partners who are participating in mediation.[3] Thus, one prominent mediator (Haynes, 1988) describes a divorce mediation case in which "the man was physically and emotionally powerful, but was reduced to tears by the thought that his wife might deprive him of access to his children" (p.1).

So-called deviant cases such as this are routinely experienced by many, if not most, family mediators.[4] Collectively, their everyday working experience indicates that power imbalances at the level of societal aggregates (gender groups) are not invariably reproduced at the level of individual males and females participating in the process of divorce mediation. In other words, although a power imbalance favoring males may exist at the level of society—males run political, economic, educational, religious, legal, and military institutions—males as individuals may be more, equally, or less powerful than the individual female partners from whom they are separating.

Theoretical developments in social science have moved away from reducing marital power relations in families to gender stratification in society, to theorizing about possible or probable societal and family linkages (Alexander, Giesen, Munch, & Smelser, 1987; Schelling, 1978). In their theory of marital power, Blumberg and Coleman (1989) link levels of gender power relations through the concept of *discount factors* (pp. 233-236). Thus, a male may be a member of a gender group earning over one third more than females and an individual who earns twice as much as his wife, but his greater income—a power resource— may not be transformed into an equivalent degree of persuasive strength (power in use) because of the operation of such discount factors as his greater commitment to the marital relationship (she may leave if he attempts to control her too often or too much), her relative youth and greater physical attractiveness (she has more alternative males with which to establish a relationship), and their shared commitment to gender equality.

Discount factors operate in stable marital relationships as well as those that are in transition.[5] As a process, separation or divorce is associated with changes that do not merely discount the power of males but may actually reverse gender imbalances in marital power. This possibility tends to be ignored by some feminist critics of mediation. It is also a possibility that most husbands whose wives made the decision to separate or divorce must face (Hopper, 1992), for in the majority of cases, the decision to separate or divorce is made by female partners (Ellis, 1994).

Separation or divorce is a process that begins when the couple are still married and/or living together. Analysis of qualitative data collected by Ellis (1994, 1995), as well as the findings of Bowker (1983), Gondolph and Fisher (1988), and Schwartz (1988, 1989), strongly suggest that the female partner's decision to separate is an expression, not of "learned helplessness," but of "learned strength."[6] Diane Neumann (1992), a mediator who describes herself as an ardent feminist, contends that changes in spousal power dynamics often favoring female partners are associated with their decision to separate (p. 223).

A third possibility, one that is also ignored by critics of mediation, is that the anxiety, uncertainty, and stress of separation provide a unique opportunity for mediators to redress spousal power imbalances. According to Neumann (1992), separation creates a condition of crisis that increases the effectiveness of mediator attempts aimed at neutralizing spousal power differences.

In Neumann's account, the interaction between the divorce crisis and the ability of the mediator to intervene in ways that neutralize the effect of spousal power differences helps the spouses themselves to reach fair agreements. In Bottomley's account, any separating female who is participating in mediation does not have the capacity to bargain as an equal because she is a member of a subordinate gender group. The male with whom she is bargaining will *necessarily* have greater potential power because of his greater command over economic, psychological, and other relevant resources. In use, his greater power will reliably yield outcomes he favors, prevent her from obtaining outcomes she prefers, or yield outcomes both favor.

Conceptions of Power: Lever Versus Process

A critical evaluation of these two accounts, as well as many others that are not unlike them, yields the following conclusions. First, power and therefore power imbalances have not been adequately conceptualized. For example, in their otherwise excellent book, Folberg and Taylor (1984) refer to inequalities in power between separating spouses as an outcome or condition associated with the differential possession of resources such as "information about family finances, the legal process, . . . the developmental needs of children, . . . intelligence" (p. 185). In this conception, inequality in power is inferred from inequalities in outcomes or condition. The process whereby resources (potential power) are converted or transformed into spousal persuasive strength is ignored. Instead, Folberg and Taylor offer a *power-as-lever* conception in which the differential possession of resources is equated with differences in persuasive strength (power in use), and inequalities in power are known only when outcomes are known. Similar conceptions are either offered by, or are implicit in, the writings of Benjamin and Irving (1993), Davis and Roberts (1989), Davis and Salem (1984), Haynes (1981), Kressel, Deutch, Jaffe, Tuchman, & Watson, (1977) and Parkinson (1983).[7]

A static, nonprocessual power-as-lever conception does more than divert attention away from the process that brings about spousal convergence on the outcomes of mediation. It cannot explain this process because it entails the idea that the relative power of the spouses is only knowable when the outcomes of mediation are known. This idea is not compatible with an explanation of the process leading to spousal convergence on outcomes. A process model of power can help explain this process (Gulliver, 1979).

The starting point of the process model formulated by Gulliver is the indeterminate relation between potential power and persuasive strength. Thus, one spouse may have greater potential power (resources) and not use it, or the potential power of both spouses may be equal, and yet, in the process of interaction and bargaining, one spouse may emerge as the party with greater persuasive strength. The dynamic, emergent aspects of persuasive strength are clearly described in Gulliver's field research on mediation and Eisenberg's (1982) discussion of transactional incapacity.

The second general conclusion is that systematically collected empirical evidence supporting the positions of Bottomley and Neumann is not cited. The longitudinal study conducted by Ellis (1994) represents an attempt to provide such evidence.

Research Hypotheses

- ▥ There are statistically significant differences in power between separating male and female partners participating in mediation, and these differences favor males.
- ▥ Gender differences in power favoring male partners are reliably associated with outcomes that are markedly unfair to female partners participating in mediation.
- ▥ The effects of gender differences in power favoring male partners on the fairness of outcomes is mediated by the ability and motivation of the mediator to neutralize or redress the mediation process.

Gender and Power Imbalances: Marital

The first hypothesis was tested using a number of indicators of power. Following Blood and Wolfe (1960) and Scanzoni (1965), we assumed that differences in persuasive strength (power) would be reflected in decisions made by husbands and wives during their marriages. Pretesting revealed the existence of a number of decisions that most separating partners made during their marital relationship. An analysis of qualitative data, including couple data, indicated that the partners themselves did not rank these decisions according to their significance or importance.[8] We are not suggesting they are all equally important to husbands and wives but only that the husbands and wives in our separating sample did not rank them. Findings on marital decision making are presented in Table 6.1.

This table shows that there was considerable variation across specific items. Thus, 84.3% of males and 58.9% of females in the comparison sample reported making their own decisions about their employment. On the other hand, 50.8% of the females and 5.9% of the males reported making decisions about the education of their children. A higher proportion of males also reported making decisions about their

Table 6.1 Power-Control Imbalances, by Sample and Sex

	Sample					
	Males (by Percentage)			Females (by Percentage)		
Decisions[a]	Me	Partner	Both	Me	Partner	Both
Money	12.1	22.7	65.2	22.3	42.0	35.7
My employment	84.3	1.4	14.3	58.9	19.6	21.5
Moving	12.3	12.3	75.4	18.5	30.5	51.0
Have children	8.9	14.3	76.8	17.6	9.2	73.1
Number of children	8.2	30.6	61.2	28.6	18.5	52.9
My friends	40.9	25.8	33.3	28.8	40.8	31.2
Sex	12.7	16.9	70.4	12.0	38.0	50.0
Education of children	5.9	21.6	72.5	50.8	7.4	41.8
Vacations	5.0	11.7	83.3	16.3	32.5	51.2
All decisions: averages	21.1	17.5	61.4	28.2	26.5	45.4

NOTE: Family Mediation Pilot project sample (Ellis, 1994): N = 363; males, n = 82; females, n = 179.
a. Figures track responses to the following question: Listed below are a number of statements about how couples who are married or live together make decisions about various things. For each of these, please indicate who made the decision in your relationship.

friends and the friends of their partners (40.9% and 25.8% vs. 28.8% and 40.8%). However, 22.3% of females and 12.1% of males reported making their own decisions about money. In sum, males appear to have had greater decision-making power with respect to employment and friends. Female partners reported having greater decision-making power with respect to moving, having children, the number of children, children's education, and vacations. At the same time, examination of male-female differences on the entire set of decisions reveals no significant differences in the averages reported by them for "me" and "partner" decisions. There is a significant difference in the averages reported for "both" decisions, with males being more likely than females to report joint decision making.

The next step in the analysis involved examining marital decisions made by abused and nonabused females in the mediation and lawyer samples. Among the former, statistically significant differences were found for moving, friends, vacations, and sex. Compared with non-abused females, significantly higher proportions of abused females reported that their male partners made the decisions about these four items (see Table 6.2).

Among females in the lawyer sample, statistically significant differences were found for money, employment, moving, friends, and vacations. Compared with nonabused female lawyer clients, significantly higher proportions of abused female lawyer clients reported that their male partners made the decisions about these five items.

Males in both mediation and lawyer samples also reported being abused by their female partners. An examination of the association between abuse toward males and marital decision making reveals that there are no statistically significant differences between them. In other words, approximately equal proportions of abused and nonabused males in both samples answered "me," "partner," and "both" to all nine items included in Table 6.2.

These findings indicate that the use of one power resource, abuse, is associated with gender asymmetry favoring males in marital decision making among females in the lawyer and mediation samples. Wife abuse, it seems, mediates the effect of masculinity on marital decision making. Husband abuse, however, does not mediate the effect of femininity on marital decision making.

Gender and Power Imbalances: Postmarital

The final step in this specific analysis involved regressing abused-non-abused (as well as years of education, income, and marital decisions) on outcomes (custody, access, support, and property arrangements). Abused-nonabused was found not to be a statistically significant predictor of outcomes among wives in the lawyer and mediation samples and husbands in the mediation sample. There were too few husbands in the lawyer sample ($n = 25$) to carry out the same sort of analysis on them.

Assuming that gender differences in marital power are likely to be reflected in male and female partner estimates of their ability and motivation to use their power resources in bargaining, we asked them a question designed to measure these self-estimates. This question was, "At present (i.e., immediately prior to participating in mediation), if

Table 6.2 Marital Decisions by Sample and Presence or Absence of Abuse

Decisions	Lawyer Clients[a] (by Percentage)				Mediation Clients[b] (by Percentage)			
	Abused		Nonabused		Abused		Nonabused	
	Me	Partner	Me	Partner	Me	Partner	Me	Partner
Money	23.9	53.3	33.8	29.0[*]	20.0	44.4	16.6	40.0
My employment	50.0	32.9	64.0	12.0[**]	66.0	12.8	58.6	10.3
Moving	24.0	33.3	17.7	11.1[**]	10.6	42.6	6.9	20.7[*]
Have children	23.4	10.9	14.6	9.8	8.6	5.0	13.6	0.0
Number of children	31.3	26.9	28.6	17.1	34.3	12.8	28.0	4.0
My friends	23.9	48.9	30.9	20.4[**]	22.7	54.5	48.3	31.0[*]
Education of children	56.7	11.9	58.8	5.9	45.0	9.0	44.0	0.0
Vacations	9.8	55.7	17.5	22.5[**]	17.1	34.2	16.0	8.0[*]
Sex	8.3	44.0	8.3	27.0	10.0	50.0	18.0	21.4[*]

NOTE: The sample was all female.
a. $n = 79$.
b. $n = 102$.
c. Figures track responses to the following question: Listed below are a number of statements about how couples who are married or live together make decisions about various things. For each of these, please indicate who made the decision in your relationship.
[*]$p < .05$; [**]$p < .01$

there is a disagreement, how well can you stand up for yourself and state your own position, compared with your partner?" When the responses of male and female partners were compared, no significant differences were found. Specifically, 39% of males versus 36% of females reported "better," 44% versus 39% reported "equally well," and 18% versus 26% reported "less well." Abused wives in the mediation sample are as likely as nonabused wives to fall into the better or equally well response categories.

Another measure of premediation imbalances in potential power is differences in education (Folberg & Taylor, 1984). We found that this power resource is equally distributed among male and female partners.

Specifically, 38.6% of males and 37.2% of females reported having received an undergraduate or graduate education. Approximately equal proportions graduated from high school. In addition to equality with respect to their general educational backgrounds, male and female partners in the mediation sample were equally well educated legally. That is to say, they participated equally in Family Law Information Meetings prior to mediation. These were held twice a month and were designed to legally educate separating partners.

A number of mediators and researchers identify income as an important power resource (Blumberg & Coleman, 1989; Davis & Salem, 1984; Folberg & Taylor, 1984; Parkinson, 1983; Ricci, 1985).[9] In our sample of separating couples, there is a difference between the monthly income levels of male and female partners: Almost 54% of male and less than one third (30%) of female partners reported monthly earnings of $2,000 or more. This difference is statistically significant ($p<.05$). Income however, was not found to be a statistically significant predictor of any of the major outcomes of the study (e.g., access arrangements, child support levels, property division, custody). Moreover, it was not found to be a statistically significant predictor of the one outcome favoring males in the mediation sample over their counterparts in the lawyer sample: This was joint custody. In interpreting this finding, it is relevant to note that the mediation clients in our sample did have to pay the lawyers who provided them with legal advice or reviewed their mediation agreements. Only the mediation sessions and legal consultant fees were paid for out of public funds.

Having discovered approximate equality in potential power—except for differences in income and size or strength—we then turned our attention to how mediators addressed this situation. This was done by examining the responses of mediation clients to the following question: "Looking back on the mediation you have just completed, which of the following best describes your mediator?" More than 81% (61 of 77) of female clients reported "did not take sides," 15.8% reported "took my partner's side," and 2.6% reported "took my side." The comparable figures for male mediation clients are 71.2%, 24.5%, and 3.4%, respectively.

From the perspective of male and female partners, then, mediators were conforming with the norm of neutrality. Conformity with this norm does not necessarily mean the absence of attempts to neutralize or redress imbalances in power, potential or actual (Folberg & Taylor,

1984). Such attempts could have been made but were not perceived as neutrality violations by participants. In any event, mediator neutrality, with or without support for the weaker party, was found to coexist with gender differences in the perceived fairness of custody arrangements. A significantly higher proportion of female partners were unhappy with joint custody.

This finding stands in an ambiguous relationship to the third hypothesis (Neumann, 1992). Mediator support for the weaker party could have mediated the effects of income and other power resource differences favoring males on outcomes, but we have no direct and independent measures of this other than orientations toward advocacy in favor of the weaker party communicated to us by mediators during interviews with them. There was little variation here, so there was no point in cross-tabulating mediator orientation with the perceived fairness of outcomes. On the other hand, this finding does not support Bottomley's assertion that mediator neutrality facilitates the process of reaching agreements favoring joint custody and, therefore, males.

As an outcome, joint custody is favored by a higher proportion of male partners. As long as both partners are perceived as equally motivated and capable parents, however, neither their other potential resources, mediator neutrality, nor mediator empowerment of the weaker party is as important a predictor of joint custody as the professional values of mediators. They value joint custody over sole and split custody arrangements because they believe it is in the best interests of the children and of the family as a whole. Female partners view joint custody as unfair because most believe (correctly) that they would have been awarded sole custody had they hired a lawyer and gone to court.

The issue of joint custody is relevant to a more general consideration of the part played by mediator agendas and mediator power in bringing about convergence on outcomes they value.

Mediators as Brokers

Following Gulliver (1979), we conceive of mediators as brokers rather than "pure service professionals" (i.e., professionals acting as alter egos for separating partners). According to Kritzer (1990), pure service professionals "work solely in the interests of their clients with no . . . interests of their own" (p. 12). Brokers, on the other hand, are intermediaries who work in the interests of their clients but who also have "a set of interests that intervenes on, or even conflicts with, the goal of pure service" (p. 12).[10] A professional's agenda is a plan that includes major values and objectives, as well as ways of achieving them, that are derived from a systematic body of knowledge. Mediators are brokers with agendas, and they attempt to use their resources (potential power) in ways that bring about a convergence on some of the outcomes they prefer.

Figure 6.1 describes a process model of power that is applicable to both male and female partners participating in mediation and to the mediator.

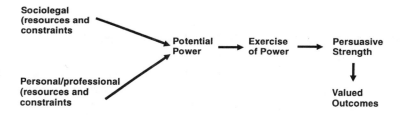

Figure 6.1. Process Model of Power

In this figure, resources refer to anything, material or normative, that increases the potential power of partners as bargainers and of mediators as brokers. *Material resources* include money, property, physical size, and strength. *Normative resources* refer to norms and values that can be called on to legitimize claims or grievances and bargaining positions.

Sociological resources refer to resources whose source can be traced to society as a whole (e.g., values and norms shared by most members of society), its legal (criminal and civil) system, or both. To say that mediation takes place in the shadow of society and the law (Mnookin, 1979) is to emphasize the resources offered and the constraints imposed by society and the law. Thus, a female partner who has been mainly responsible for caring for the children and placing their needs over her career interests may be able to call on a normative resource (conformity with societal norms and values constitutive of a good parent) in bargaining for sole custody and her consequent lack of, or low, income from employment in bargaining for a higher level of child support. Legal contingencies include having to go to court to settle issues that could not be settled through the process of mediation. In addition to a loss of control over the dispute-settling process, this entails increased costs, delay, and uncertainty over outcomes.

The attempts by each spouse to persuade the other to behave in ways that conform to the norms and values supporting their respective preferences coexist with attempts by mediators to persuade both spouses to conform to norms and values that are important to mediators as professionals. According to Silbey and Merry (1986), one significant professional value mediators impose on spouses participating in mediation is "the validity of the language of relationships for representing parties' grievances" (p. 26).[11] This process, as well as the persuasive strength of mediators generally, is facilitated when mediators engage in *shuttle mediation,* the practice of alternating sessions with individual spouses with sessions including both together. Other things being equal, the higher the ratio of alternating individual to joint sessions, the higher the persuasive strength of mediators and the lower the persuasive strength of the spouses, individually and jointly. The mechanisms underlying the greater persuasive strength of mediators are control over communication and, therefore, control over matters of substance, such as which specific issues are put forward and in what order (Silbey & Merry, 1986).

The legal setting or context for mediation also offers resources and imposes constraints. For example, in jurisdictions where *open mediation* is permitted (i.e., mediators' reports or mediation agreements can be used in litigation), mediators are offered an important power resource that is denied to those practicing in jurisdictions where only *closed mediation* is permitted, in which reports and agreements cannot be used in litigation. Another example is the authoritative "halo" of the court as a resource that is available to court-based mediators but not to those in private practice (Ogus, Walker, & Jones-Lee, 1989). Last, mandatory mediation may offer mediators resources that are not available to those participating in mediation with voluntary clients (Grillo, 1991).

Personal resources include general intelligence, relevant knowledge, experience in bargaining, size, strength, impulse control, insight, empathy, patience, gender, race-ethnicity, personality, and training as well as experience in settling conflicts. We also conceive of one partner's knowledge of the real or true preference of the other for different outcomes (e.g., sole custody, liberal access, adequate child support payments) as a personal power resource. Thus, a male partner who knows his female partner values sole custody of their children above all other outcomes can use this knowledge in the following way: He can ask for joint custody (as a tactic) and then agree to sole custody for the mother in return for liberal access and reduced child support payments. Conversely, mothers who have interim custody and know their partners don't want sole custody but do value liberal access arrangements very highly can use this knowledge in bargaining for adequate child support payments.

Potential power is determined by the quantity, quality, and availability of sociolegal, personal, and professional resources. Net potential power refers to potential power minus "discounts"—situational or relational factors that either decrease the quantity, quality, or both of potential power resources or decrease the motivation or ability to transform them into persuasive strength.

The exercise of power, or power used in the context of interaction, converts potential power into actual power (persuasive strength). Threatening, promising, informing, manipulating, misinforming, compromising, cooperating, exchanging, coercing, revealing where the best interests of the other party or parties truly lie, appealing to higher loyalties (such as the best interest of the children), referring to societal norms and values or the norms and values of significant social groupings, and revealing the underlying causes of spousal or parental conflicts are all ways of exercising power.

Control over the process of communication has been identified as one of the most significant factors influencing the exercise of power in mediation (Davis & Roberts, 1989; Gulliver, 1979; Schelling, 1969). According to Davis and Roberts (1989), mediator control over the process of communication is essential to realizing the objective of ensuring that the weaker partner can effectively bargain as an equal. The tactics used by mediators to establish and maintain control of communication and the resources available to them have been described by Davis and Roberts (1989), Davis and Salem (1984), Folberg and Taylor (1984), Grillo (1991), and Silbey and Merry (1986). Mediator control over client behavior is facilitated by the fact that separating partners are often in a state of crisis (Neumann, 1992) and are strangers to both the mediation process and the norms governing interaction during mediation sessions (Grillo, 1991).

Differences in the effective exercise of power are reflected in differences in the persuasive strength of each partner and the mediator. Their relative persuasive strength is indicated by a convergence on outcomes of mediation that are valued most highly by one, both, or all of the participants, including the mediator.

Valued outcomes of mediation have to do with custody and access arrangements (family mediation) as well as financial support and property division in comprehensive mediation.

In concluding this chapter, two sets of considerations are relevant. The first applies to the process model of power and the second to the findings presented earlier. Among mediators, valued outcomes include mediation agreements that reflect values that are important to them (e.g., shared parenting, equity), high compliance rates, continuity of the mediation service, personal satisfaction, career enhancement, and job security.

Our analysis of mediator power differs from Silbey and Merry's (1986) useful one in a number of significant respects. First, it is grounded in an explicitly formulated conception and definition of power. Their mediator settlement strategies are explicitly grounded in neither. Second, our starting point is mediators with power resources. Silbey and Merry's mediators do not have, or appear not to have, power resources available to them. Third, our model can explain variations in the persuasive strength of mediators. Their discussion focuses exclusively on the persuasive strength of mediators, but they cannot account for variations in their persuasive strength. In the Silbey and Merry process model, mediators with "no power" (pp. 7-8) are able to impose the language of relationships for representing disputants' grievances "on the disputants, and also settle conflicts through the exercise of power" (p. 27). Is this equally true of all mediators? More generally, if mediators are so powerful, why are full agreements reached in only 30% to 40% and not in 80% to 90% of mediated cases? (Ellis, 1994).[12] Last, settlement strategies (presentation of self and program, control of mediation process, control of substantive issues, and activation of commitments) constitute Silbey and Merry's model of mediator power but represent only one part (persuasive strength) of our power model.

The process model of power presented here also applies to lawyers. This conclusion is supported by the work of Kritzer (1990), who conceives of lawyers as brokers, and the research of Galanter (1981), Griffiths (1986), O'Gorman (1963), Rosenthal (1974), Sarat and Felstiner (1986), and others on how lawyers actually do lawyering.[13]

A comparison of power imbalances in mediation and family lawyering reveals that power imbalances between lawyers and clients are greater than those between mediators and their clients. Moreover, as lawyer clients are in a better position than mediation clients to convert economic resources (potential power) into persuasive strength via the purchase of legal representation and male lawyer clients often possess greater economic resources, gender differences in potential power favoring males are frequently greater between male and female lawyer clients than between male and female mediation clients.

In evaluating the descriptive findings, three considerations ought to be kept in mind. First and foremost, partners in the mediation sample had been screened in by mediators. This means they had not detected personal, role-based, or gender-based power imbalances that, in their judgment, were great enough to adversely influence the bargaining capacity of the partners who had been abused or whose earned income was lower (or both). In addition to the implementation of abuse and power imbalance screening procedures during intake, mediators also acted as "resource expanders" for both partners but especially the weaker one.[14] That is to say, mediators provided separating partners with information about the availability of local support services that could help them bargain more effectively.

Second, economic differences between male and female partners were not as great in our sample as they may be in other samples. In them, economic inequality favoring males retaining lawyers privately may well constitute an imbalance in potential power that favors males.

Third, mediation takes place under the threat canopy of struggle. Struggles (interpersonal exchanges involving the threat or use of physical force) place a premium on physical size. Here, a clear imbalance in potential power favoring males exists. This imbalance, however, may not be unique to clients in the mediation sample. It also favors males in the lawyer sample who attempted to settle disputes with their female partners prior to hiring lawyers or while their lawyers were negotiating (or both).

Last, it is possible that mediation process-relevant power imbalances favoring males were present, but our questions and the mediators' did not detect them. In reply, we admit as other researchers would that questions we did not ask, or questions we did ask but in the wrong way, may vitiate the findings. At the same time, we did attempt to measure power imbalances using a number of different questions, and these yielded consistent results. Third, perusal of unsolicited comments made by clients and recorded verbatim in the questionnaire revealed no evidence indicating that mediation process-relevant power imbalances were subjectively experienced or that they adversely influenced the capacity of female partners to bargain as equals. Power imbalances may well exist in our sample of mediation clients despite our best efforts to detect them, but those who insist on them even after screening may well be hurting rather than helping women, especially battered women, who are separating from their partners.

In this specific connection, feminist lawyer Martha Mahoney (1991) notes the following:

> In contested custody decisions . . . women are . . . at risk that either too much strength or too little strength may be held against them. . . . The portrait of battered women as pathologically weak—the court's version of what feminists have told them—may disservice mothers seeking custody." (p. 4)

Essentially, the same warning is stated by another feminist, Phyllis Chesler (1986), in her book *Mothers on Trial: The Battle for Children and Custody*. In sum, the structuralist thesis that holds that structural sources of gender inequality inevitably create interpersonal inequalities that disadvantage female partners participating in mediation is one that is politically disadvantageous for women because it denies them the capacity to make choices and act in terms of them. It is also legally disadvantageous because judges who believe it may make decisions that run counter to women's interests and what they believe is the well-being of their children.

Summary of Findings

Gender differences in marital power vary across issues, with wives making the decisions about moving, having children, and the children's education and husbands making the decisions about employment, money, and friends.

Compared with nonabused wives, a significantly higher proportion of abused wives reported that their partners made the decisions about moving, friends, and vacations.

Compared with nonabused wives in the lawyer sample, a significantly higher proportion of abused wives reported that their partners made the decisions about money, their wives' employment, moving, wives' friends, and vacations.

Compared with nonabused wives in the mediation sample, a significantly higher proportion of abused wives in the same sample reported that their partners made decisions about moving, wives' friends, vacations, and sex.

Approximately equal proportions of abused and nonabused husbands reported that their wives made the decisions about money, employment, moving, having children, the number of children, friends, children's education, vacations, and sex.

Among wives but not husbands, marital power varied with spousal abuse.

Immediately prior to commencing mediation, approximately equal proportions of husbands and wives reported being equally or better able to stand up for themselves and state their positions (41% vs. 37%).

Equal proportions of abused and nonabused wives in the mediation sample reported being equally or better able than their partners in their ability to stand up for themselves and state their positions.

The power resource of education (university degree) was distributed equally between husbands and wives (39% vs. 37%).

The power resource of income was unequally distributed between husbands and wives, with a significantly higher proportion of husbands earning an annual median income of $24,000 or more.

Among mediation participants, husband-wife differences in income and marital power are not statistically significant predictors of differences in custody, access, support, or property arrangements.

A higher proportion of husbands than wives used the power resource of physical and psychological abuse against their partners, but their (wife) abuse was not found to be a statistically significant predictor of custody, access, support, or property arrangements.

Conclusions

- Husbands who abuse their wives have greater persuasive strength (marital power).
- Wives who abuse their husbands do not have greater persuasive strength (marital power).
- Among mediation clients participating in a divorce mediation process with an effective screening protocol and consistent monitoring of abusive behavior, imbalances in marital power are unrelated to imbalances in the outcomes of mediation.

Notes

1. See Bottomley (1984), Fischer et al. (1993), Grillo (1991), Ontario Association of Interval and Transition Houses (1989), Pagelow (1993), and Stallone (1984).

2. See Anon (1995), Pierson and Cohen (1994), Wiener and Gunderson (1990), and Brockman and Chunn (1993).

3. For a more detailed description of the basis of spousal power differences among mediation participants, see Davis and Roberts (1989) and Haynes (1988).

4. This is a view expressed by the mediators participating in the Family Mediation Pilot Project (Ellis, 1994). See also Haynes (1988).

5. Blumberg and Coleman's (1989) discussion of relationships in transition does not cover transitions associated with separation or divorce. Transition is associated with a decrease in the net income of male partners.

6. Both Gondolf and Fisher (1988) and Schwartz (1989) provide findings that refute Walker's (1979) concept of *learned helplessness* (pp. 49-50).

7. For theory and research on marital power, see Blumberg and Coleman (1989), Chafetz (1980), Cromwell and Olson (1975), Huber and Spitze (1983), McDonald (1980), and Scanzoni (1982).

8. Scanzoni (1965) and Turk and Bell (1972) have written useful articles on the measurement of marital power.

9. Blumberg and Coleman (1989) reported findings indicating that spousal differences in income are far stronger predictors of differences in marital power than are spousal differences in violence.

10. These types are being treated as categories for analytical purposes. Empirically, mediators (and lawyers) may be placed on a continuum with pure professionals at one end and pure brokers at the other. It is also likely that any given mediator (or lawyer) may act as a pure professional with respect to one issue (e.g., access) and a broker to another one (e.g., custody).

11. Bush and Folger (1994) cite evidence indicating that divorce mediators are also quite willing to impose agreements on separating or divorcing spouses.

12. Bush and Folger (1994) may have had Silbey and Merry (1986) in mind when they summarized criticisms of mediation under the title *The Oppression Story*.

13. See also Cavanagh and Rhode (1976) and Felstiner, Abel, and Sarat (1980-1981).

14. The role of mediators as resource expanders is discussed in some detail by Stulberg and Bridenback (1981).

Issues and Outcomes

The Hamilton Unified Family Court's mediation service was a comprehensive one. As such, it mediated issues of custody, access, support, and property division. When clients in the mediation and lawyer samples were asked, "Which issues did you bring to mediation?" more than two thirds (68.7%) in the comparison sample (i.e., the sample prior to the commencement of mediation or lawyer negotiation) answered, "Access" (see Table 7.1). Close to 40% wanted the issues of custody and child support settled. The smallest fraction, about one tenth, wanted the issue of spousal support settled (Ellis, 1994).

Table 7.1 also presents the results of subsample comparisons. For females in the mediation and lawyer samples, the major findings are these. First, the highest proportion of females in the mediation sample (69.2%) wanted the issue of access settled. Second, the highest proportion of females in the lawyer sample (63.7%) wanted the issue of child support settled. Third, compared with females in the mediation sample, a significantly higher proportion of females in the lawyer sample wanted the issue of child support settled (63.7% vs. 47.4%). Fourth, sample differences on other issues are not great.

Table 7.1 Issues in Contention, by Sample and Sex

| | Samples | | | | | | |
| | Total | Females | | Mediation | | Total | |
Issues	All $(n = 263)^a$	Mediation $(n = 77)$	Lawyer $(n = 102)$	Males $(n = 57)$	Females $(n = 77)$	Males $(n = 82)$	Females $(n = 179)$
Spousal support	10.7	14.3	23.9	5.3	14.3	4.7	15.1
Child support	38.7	47.4	63.7	31.0	47.4	30.8	44.7
Custody	39.6	40.0	29.4	43.1	40.0	43.1	36.9
Access	68.7	69.2	52.0	74.1	69.2	70.8	67.1
Property division	32.0	27.4	39.2	27.6	27.4	27.7	35.3

a. Males and females in the comparison sample do not sum to 263 because sex was not coded for respondents.

The proportion of males and females in the mediation sample who brought the issues of spousal support (5.3% vs. 14.3%), custody (43.1% vs. 40.0%), access (74.1% vs. 69.2%), and property division (27.6% vs. 27.4%) to mediation were not significantly different. The proportions bringing the issue of child custody were significantly different (31.0% for males and 47.4% for females).

A comparison between male and female partners (comparison sample) yields the following major findings. First, access is the issue in contention for the highest proportion of both males (70.8%) and females (67.1%). Second, a higher proportion of females wanted the issue of child support settled (44.7% vs. 30.8%). Third, male-female differences on the other issues are not significant.

The issues brought to lawyers and mediators for settlement were associated with different degrees of contention or disagreement for females in the mediation and lawyer samples. Comparisons presented in Table 7.2 yield these major findings: First, a higher proportion of females in the mediation sample reported serious to very serious disagreements over the issue of child support (83.7% vs. 69.4%) prior to the start of the legal processing of their separations. Second, the

Table 7.2 Seriousness of Disagreements Over Issues, by Sample and Sex

	Samples						
	Comparison	Females		Mediation		Comparison	
Issues	All (n = 263)[a]	Mediation (n = 77)	Lawyer (n = 102)	Males (n = 57)	Females (n = 77)	Males (n = 82)	Females (n = 179)
Access	76.6	74.3	87.5	69.4	74.3	63.8	85.7
Custody	73.3	81.3	70.3	64.5	81.3	72.9	73.2
Child support	73.5	83.7	69.4	63.6	83.7	69.0	75.2
Property division	74.3	75.0	72.4	76.9	75.0	75.0	73.8

NOTE: The figures represent the percentage who reported the disagreements as *very serious* or *serious* to the question, "How serious are the disagreements (with your partner) over these issues?"
a. Males and females in the comparison sample do not sum to 263 because sex was not coded for respondents.

proportions of females in the two samples reporting serious disagreements over the remaining issues were not significantly different.

Comparisons between males and females in the mediation sample reveal that significantly higher proportions of females reported serious disagreement over the issue of child support (83.7% vs. 63.6%) and custody (81.3% vs. 64.5%). The proportions of males and females reporting serious disagreements over the remaining issues prior to commencing mediation were not significantly different.

A comparison between males and females yields these major findings: First, a significantly higher proportion of females reported serious to very serious disadvantages over the issue of access (85.7% vs. 63.8%). Second, sample differences between males and females in the seriousness of disagreements on the other issues are not significant.

Another indicator of the seriousness of disagreements over issues in contention is client expectations of litigation. When they were asked, "Do you think you will have to go to court and have a judge settle the issue (you want settled)?," the highest proportion (43.7%) replied, "Yes" over the issue of child support. Approximately one quarter (23%) gave the same response to the issues of custody, access, and property division.

For females in the lawyer and mediation samples, the proportions replying "yes" to the question for all four issues was not significantly different (52.7% vs. 45.9% over child support, 20.5% vs. 19.7% over custody, 21.9% vs. 32.8% over access, and 20.5% vs. 21.3% over property division). For the mediation sample, the only significant difference between male and female clients was the proportion expecting to have to go to court to have the issue of child support settled (28.9% vs. 45.9%, respectively). This was also the only significant difference between males and females in the comparison sample. Here, a higher proportion of females expected to have to let a judge settle the issue (49.6% vs. 31.1%).

A third indicator of seriousness of disagreements is the amount of time partners spent trying to settle the issues in contention. For all four issues combined, the average time devoted to trying to settle them by all clients (comparison sample) was 8.2 months. The largest period of time, 10 months, was devoted to trying to settle the issues of access and property division. Settlement efforts directed at the issue of custody and child support had been going on for 6 and 7 months, respectively.

Compared with females in the lawyer sample, females in the mediation sample had spent twice as many months in total attempting to settle the issue of access (12 months vs. 6 months) and more than twice as many months trying to settle the issue of custody (11 months vs. 5 months). The average number of months that females in the lawyer sample had been attempting to settle the issues of child support and property division was higher than the comparable figure for mediation clients (10 months vs. 7 months and 12 months vs. 7 months, respectively). For all four issues combined, female mediation clients had been attempting to settle them for an average of 9.3 months; the comparable figure for females in the lawyer sample is 8.3 months.

For all four issues combined, male and female clients in the comparison sample had been attempting to settle them for an average of 8 months. The difference between males and females is greatest with respect to the average time devoted to the issues of access and property division. Males reported devoting almost twice the amount of time to settling the issue of property division (11 months vs. 7 months).

In addition to specific questions, clients were also asked about what custody arrangements and child support dollar amounts they wanted. They were asked these questions prior to commencing mediation or lawyer negotiations. After their separations had been processed, they were asked to identify the custody arrangements and child support dollar amounts they had received or to which they had agreed. Their answers to both questions were then cross-tabulated.

Among females in the lawyer sample, 75 (78.1%) had asked for sole custody and 64 (85%) of them obtained sole custody. Of the 21 (29.1%) who had not asked for sole custody, none obtained it. This "wanted-got" relationship is statistically significant ($p<.001$). Among females in the mediation sample, 61 (81.3%) had asked for sole custody and 47 (67.2%) of them obtained it. For these clients, the wanted-got relationship is also statistically significant ($p<.001$).

Compared with females in the mediation sample, a markedly higher proportion of females in the lawyer sample wanted and got sole custody of their children (85.0% vs. 67.2%); this difference is statistically significant ($p<.001$). One possible explanation of this difference is the relatively high proportion of male mediation clients who wanted joint physical custody. Thus, whereas only 3 out of 21 (14.3%) male lawyer clients wanted this custody arrangement, 31 of 57 (51.7%) male mediation clients wanted it.

For females in the mediation sample, the median dollar amount wanted in monthly child support payments was $600.00. The corresponding figure for females in the lawyer sample was $500.00. For female mediation clients, the monthly support payments asked for ranged from $100.00 to $1,500. The corresponding figures for female lawyer clients were $100.00 to $2,000. Included among those asking for the highest monthly child support payments were three asking for $1,500.00 or more. These findings indicate that female mediation clients asked for higher monthly child support payments than female lawyer clients.

Females in the mediation and lawyer samples also reported the dollar amounts for child support they had agreed to or settled for. Among the former, 33 (70.2%) asked for $600.00 or more per month and 26 (78.8%) obtained this amount. Fourteen (29.8%) asked for less, and 12 of them agreed to accept less than $600.00 per month. This wanted-got relationship is statistically significant ($p < .001$).

Among females in the lawyer sample, 34 (52.3%) asked for $500.00 or more per month and 23 (67.7%) obtained this amount. Thirty-one (47.7%) asked for less and 28 (90.3%) agreed to accept less than $500.00 per month. This wanted-got relationship is also statistically significant ($p < .05$).

Compared with females in the lawyer sample, a higher proportion of females in the mediation sample got the monthly child support payments they wanted (three quarters vs. two thirds, approximately). This difference cannot be accounted for by the presence of more dependent children in the mediation sample. In fact, the average number of children is almost the same in the two samples (1.6 for female mediation and 1.5 for female lawyer clients).

Differences in income probably explain why female mediation clients asked for or wanted higher monthly child support payments. Specifically, 54% of males in the mediation sample but only 42% of males in the lawyer sample earned monthly incomes of $2,000.00 or more per month. Females in the lawyer sample were also poorer. More than 90% earned less than $2,000.00 per month as compared with 70.0% in the mediation sample. Their economic needs may have been as pressing, but they did not ask for the higher amounts asked for by female mediation clients because of their appraisal or acknowledgment of their partner's inability to pay them.

In an attempt to assess the effects of possible or probable power imbalances we may have failed to measure, the wanted-got relationship for child support payments among males in the mediation sample was also analyzed. Thirteen (40.6%) wanted to make payments of $600.00 or more per month and all of them agreed to this. Nineteen (59.4%) wanted to pay less than $600.00 per month and 16 (84.2%) of them got what they wanted. That is to say, their partners agreed to accept less than $600.00 per month in child support payments. This relationship is statistically significant ($p < .001$). These findings, when compared with those of females in the mediation sample, indicate that there are no significant differences in the wanted-got relationship among male and female mediation clients.[1]

Summary of Findings

Among females in the mediation sample, the highest proportion (69.2%) wanted the issue of access settled.

Among females in the lawyer sample, the highest proportion (63.7%) wanted the issue of child support settled.

A higher proportion of females in the lawyer sample than in the mediation sample wanted the issue of child support settled (63.7% vs. 47.4%).

Compared with females in the lawyer sample, a higher proportion of females in the mediation sample reported very serious to serious disagreements over the issue of child support (83.7% vs. 69.4%) prior to commencing the legal processing of their separations.

The proportion of males and females in the mediation sample who brought the issues of custody, access, and property division to mediation were not significantly different.

Compared with other issues, the highest proportion of all clients (comparison sample—43.7%) expected to have to litigate the issue of child support.

The proportion who expected to have to go to court to settle issues in contention was similar for females in the mediation and lawyer samples.

Compared with female mediation clients, a significantly higher proportion of males in the mediation sample reported serious disagreements over the issue of child support (83.7% vs. 63.6%) and custody (81.3% vs. 64.5%).

Compared with males in the mediation sample, a significantly higher proportion of female mediation clients expected to have to go to court and let a judge settle the issue of child support (45.9% vs. 28.9%).

Compared with females in the lawyer sample, females in the mediation sample reported spending twice as much time trying to settle the issues of custody and access (11 months vs. 5 months and 12 months vs. 6 months, respectively) and less time trying to settle the issues of child support (7 months vs. 12 months) prior to commencing lawyer negotiations.

Compared with males in the mediation sample, female mediation clients reported spending less time trying to settle the issue of access (9.5 months vs. 13 months) prior to commencing mediation.

Compared with females in the mediation sample, a significantly higher proportion of females in the lawyer sample got the (sole) custody arrangement they wanted (85.0% vs. 67.2%).

Compared with females in the lawyer sample, a higher proportion of females in the mediation sample got the monthly child support payments they wanted (78.8% vs. 67.6%).

Conclusions

- Compared with other issues in contention, child support conflicts are perceived by both male and female partners to be least likely to be settled by either mediation or lawyer negotiations.
- Sole custody is most likely to be awarded to female partners whose separations and/or divorces are negotiated by lawyers.
- Joint custody is far more likely to be reached through mediation than through lawyer negotiations.
- Female partners participating in mediation are more likely then females involved in lawyer negotiations to get the level of child support they want.

Note

1. Because of the small number of cases ($n = 15$ to 18) in relation to the number of predictor variables included in the models, the wanted-got ratio for child support and custody was not subjected to multivariable statistical (regression) analyses.

Process, Outcomes, and Satisfaction

Process refers to a series of sequentially ordered communications aimed at bringing about a convergence on the outcomes of mediation or lawyer negotiations. The *outcomes* of mediation and lawyer negotiations include custody, access, financial support, and property division arrangements as well as the acquisition of knowledge, changes in parental communication, cooperation, and ways of resolving conflicts. The outcomes of mediation and lawyer negotiations are included in agreements and determinations, respectively. *Satisfaction* refers to evaluations of process and outcomes.

Since the mid-1970s, a number of researchers have published studies dealing with satisfaction. A few of them have controlled for process while examining the relationship between agreements (outcomes) and satisfaction, or they have controlled on agreements (outcomes) while examining the relation between process and satisfaction or both. Most have not separated satisfaction with outcomes from satisfaction with process. We shall review this body of literature with the following hypotheses in mind:

- Mediator and client satisfaction vary positively with the rate of agreements: the higher the agreement rate, the higher the proportion of satisfied mediators and clients.

▪ Client satisfaction varies with the dispute resolution process they participate in, with mediation clients being more satisfied than lawyer clients.

▪ Client satisfaction varies more with outcomes than with process: The more highly valued outcomes are to clients, the more satisfied they will be, regardless of whether the outcomes were mediated or negotiated.

Agreements and Satisfaction

In 1978, the Frontenac Family Referral Service conducted a study designed to find out "what proportion of clients could resolve [settle] the dispute(s) [they brought to mediation] through mediation" (Frontenac Family Referral Service, 1984, p. 47). Their sample comprised 81 clients with one or more issues in dispute. They found that full agreement was reached in 79% of the cases in which clients had participated in mediation prior to becoming involved with a lawyer or initiating an action (application) in court. Among clients who participated in mediation after filing an application or contacting a lawyer, the agreement rate decreased to 54%.

The Frontenac study may be one of the least costly and smallest scale studies undertaken in Canada; Richardson's (1988) Divorce Mediation in Four Canadian Cities Study is one of the largest and mostly costly. Data collected from 1,773 court files reveal that full agreement on all issues brought to mediation was achieved in 49% of the cases and a partial agreement in 15% of them. This yields an overall agreement rate of 64%. Information on agreements was also obtained from 324 clients who participated in mediation. The agreement rates they reported were a little lower: 38% reported reaching full agreement and 20% reported reaching partial agreement. This yields a client-reported agreement rate of 58%.

In 1994, Depner, Cannata, and Ricci published the results of their 1991 California Family Court Services Snapshot Study. Findings are based on 1,388 (82%) families who participated in mediation in 75 family courts spread over 51 counties. Clients in their sample were divided into two outcome groups: "reached agreement" and "impasse." Approximately 90% of clients in the former group reported being generally satisfied with mediation. The comparable figure for clients in the impasse group is 65%.

Two questions were used to measure general satisfaction: "Are you satisfied with the results of the mediation session just completed?" and "Are you satisfied with the next steps you will take?" The first question assumes that the just completed mediation session is representative of preceding ones, and the second one refers to prospective next steps rather than steps already taken. Alternative and more valid measures of general satisfaction were available to the authors (i.e., a scale or index derived from responses to "helpfulness" and four "opportunity to discuss issues" questions), but these were not used.

On the basis of responses to the two questions regarding general satisfaction they did use, Depner et al. (1994) concluded that "Reaching an agreement had the greatest impact on General Satisfaction" (p. 313). Among clients who did not reach an agreement, however, more than 90% reported that "the mediator offered good ideas," and "the procedures were clear." "Mediation was a good way to come up with a parenting plan" and that mediation "offered sufficient time and opportunity to work on issues" was reported by 80% (p. 312). Had these "helpfulness" and "opportunity to discuss" issues been included in a general satisfaction scale, the results may have undermined the validity of their conclusion.

A review of 30 or more studies by Ogus et al. (1989) and Kressel, Pruitt, and associates (1989) indicates that agreement rates (partial and full, combined) vary between 40% and 81%, with the agreement rates for access being higher than those for custody. Agreement rates were also found to vary with the timing of mediation; clients who participated in mediation shortly after they separated and before they became involved with lawyers and the court process reported higher rates of agreement.

Custody disputes were also the focus of a longitudinal study of mediation effects by Kressel et al. (1994). Over the 3-year study period, 62% (21 of 32) of the cases reached an agreement. All but three of the 32 parties—that is, more than 90% of them—reported being satisfied with the process of mediation. Kressel et al. go on to report that "more than one third of all parents who could not reach a mediated agreement [i.e., 8 of 22] were also satisfied" (p. 72). We do not know whether the 18-month postmediation telephone interviews that produced the settlement and satisfaction rates were conducted with couples. They refer to *cases, parties,* and *parents.*

Although their sample is a small one ($n = 32$ cases), the Kressel et al. (1994) study is an interesting one because they found that differences in the frequency of reaching agreements were strongly associated with mediator style. Thus, 12 of 13 couples who participated in "problem-solving mediation" reached an agreement, but only 9 of 19 who participated in "settlement-oriented mediation" did so. Moreover, reported rates of "court conflict" during the 18-month mediation period were "much lower" among those who reached agreements (p. 72).

The studies reviewed here have provided a great deal of evidence on the rate of mediated agreements but very little reliable evidence on the direction and strength of the association between this rate and either client or mediator satisfaction. For example, Pruitt, Pierce, Millicuddy, Welton, & Lynn Castrianno (1993) found that satisfaction was significantly associated with reaching an agreement ($p < .01$), but they did not also measure the association between satisfaction and *failure* to reach an agreement. This was done by Pearson and Thoennes (1984). They found that 70% of clients who reached agreements reported being satisfied. The comparable figure for those who not reach agreements was 56%. However, deviations from the experimental design, which called for the *random* assignment of clients to experimental conditions (mediation and litigation), as well as the possible selective loss of clients who were interviewed sometime after the completion of mediation and litigation, represent threats to the internal validity of their study.

Emery and Wyer's (1987b) discussions of mediation agreements suggest that the association between agreements and satisfaction is relatively complex. Thus, failure to reach an agreement may be positively associated with satisfaction for clients who become more communicative, cooperative, and educated as a result of participating in the mediation process. Failure to reach an agreement may also be positively associated with satisfaction among clients who believe, or come to believe, that the likelihood of obtaining sole custody or better access arrangements would be increased if the matter was placed in the hands of lawyers and the courts. Conversely, a high rate of agreements, especially among court-based mediators, may not be positively associated with either client or mediator satisfaction because they may be primarily a function of bureaucratic (court) pressure to dispose of cases, rather than good mediation practice.

In addition to the complexity of the relationship between mediated agreements and satisfaction, methodological problems having to do with the self-selection of sampled cases (partners who were most likely to benefit from mediation were overrepresented) and selective attrition (the loss of least satisfied and highly dissatisfied clients from among those who completed postprocessing interviews) make it difficult to draw unambiguous conclusions about the hypothesized association between agreements and satisfaction.

Mediation, Lawyer Negotiation, and Client Satisfaction

Disputes over issues arising from separation or divorce can be resolved or settled in a number of ways. These can be placed on continuum of self-determination. At the high self-determination end of the continuum would be located partners who settle or resolve matters with no, or minimal, intervention by the courts, lawyers, or mediators. Voluntary mediation, mandatory mediation, lawyer negotiations, court hearings, and trials are located at increasingly distant points from the high self-determination end, in the direction of the low end of the continuum, with the lowest point being trials. Mediators assume that client satisfaction varies directly with client self-determination. If this assumption is valid, then levels of client satisfaction should be highest among voluntary mediation clients followed by clients participating in mandatory mediation, then by those involved with lawyers who negotiate, who appear in court hearings, and who represent their clients at trials.

Since the late 1970s, Pearson and Thoennes (1984, 1988, 1989) conducted three major studies of divorce mediation. Divorce mediation programs in five sites were studied (Denver, Colorado; Minneapolis, Minnesota; Los Angeles, California; Delaware; Connecticut). Findings are based on the reports of 667 mediation clients and 189 clients participating in adversarial procedures (1989). One of their significant findings was that the level of client satisfaction did not vary with participation in voluntary or mandatory mediation. More specifically, approximately 80% of clients in both groups reported that "they would probably recommend mediation to a friend" and were "glad they tried the process" (p. 15). On the basis of these indirect measures, Pearson and Thoennes concluded that "a mandated attempted to mediate does not appear to affect . . . user satisfaction" (p. 15).

In interpreting these findings, it is important to remember that threats to self-determination can be experienced prior to and during mediation. Thus, mandatory mediation eliminates the choice of an alternative dispute resolution process, whereas pressures by a mediator to reach an agreement are experienced during the process. Clients in both the mandated and voluntary mediation groups experienced the second threat (mediator pressure), but only clients in the mandated group experienced the first threat to self-determination. This suggests that the process itself has a greater effect on client satisfaction than the route by which clients come to mediation.[1]

Other researchers who studied custody mediation have reported similar findings. Despite variations in the soundness of their research designs and the use of different outcome measures, they all reported findings indicating that mediation clients are more satisfied than adversarial clients (Emery & Wyer, 1987a).

The findings of Emery and Wyer (1986), Irving (1980), Margolin (1973), Pearson and Thoennes (1984), and Watson and Morton (1983) were based on the study of court-based custody and access (visitation) mediation. Although the samples they selected may not have been representative of this type of mediation in the settings in which it was studied, the consistency of the findings across different jurisdictions and different points in time suggests that they probably apply to court-based custody and access mediation services in general. This means they apply to the modal or predominant form of custody and access mediation (court-based) in Canada and the United States (Comeaux, 1983). But do they also apply to non-court-based, comprehensive mediation samples, such as those selected in the Divorce Mediation Project (Kelly, 1990b)?

The Divorce Mediation Project is described by Kelly (1990b) as "the only empirical, and longitudinal (2-year) study that has compared the effectiveness of an integrated, comprehensive mediation process encompassing all divorce-related issues (child custody, visiting, parenting) with an adversarial divorce process parallel in scope" (p. 3). The comprehensive mediation model described by Kelly differed from custody mediation in a number of ways, including "its voluntary non-court-connected setting" (p. 3).

The mediation sample consisted of 212 couples. This represents almost all couples (98%) whose divorces were mediated at the Northern California Mediation Center between 1983 and 1985. The adversarial sample consisted of 225 persons whose names appeared in local court records of divorce petitions filed between February 1984 and May 1986. Ninety-seven of them (43%) also agreed to participate in the study by completing interviews. The last postprocessing interview was completed 2 years following the divorce. At this time, the mediation sample was reduced to 67 participants and the adversarial sample was reduced to 160 clients.

Kelly (1990b) divided mediation clients into four outcome groups. These were "comprehensive completers" (reached written agreement on all issues; $n = 102$, 50%); "partial completers" (reached written agreement on some but not all issues; $n = 18$, 8%); "productive terminations" (did not reach a written agreement but did settle one or two major issues; $n = 32$, 15%); and "true terminations" (did not reach a written agreement and did not settle a single issue; $n = 54$, 26%).

Levels of satisfaction were found to vary with membership in these outcome groups. More specifically, completers (comprehensive and partial) were more satisfied than terminators (productive and true). The difference in level of satisfaction was statistically significant ($p<.01$). Also, mediation clients—both men and women—were more satisfied than adversarial clients; this difference is also statistically significant ($p<.01$).

Male and female mediation clients were not only more satisfied with mediation than adversarial clients were with lawyer negotiations, hearings, and trials, but they were also equally satisfied with both the process of mediation and the outcomes it produced (Kelly, 1990b). The research of Emery and Wyer (1987a) suggests that their findings may not be generalizable to custody-access mediation.

Emery and Wyer (1987b) asked 82 families who had applied to have their custody-visitation disputes heard in a local domestic relations court in Virginia to participate in their study.[2] They were to be paid for their participation (a means of decreasing sample attrition). Of these, 49 were randomly selected and asked to participate in mediation, and 35 (71%) of them agreed; 43 were asked to participate in litigation, of whom 36 (84%) agreed. The findings they reported were based on a comparison of these two randomly assigned groups. More specifically, their findings are based on interviews conducted with members of both groups approximately 5 weeks after their disputes were settled.[3]

The major findings of the Emery and Wyer (1986) study are that (a) fathers in mediation were more satisfied than mothers in litigation, (b) mothers in litigation were more satisfied than fathers in mediation, (c) fathers in litigation were the least satisfied group (i.e., they were less satisfied than mothers in mediation or litigation and fathers in mediation), and (d) mediation families were more satisfied than litigation families.

Findings on gender variations in satisfaction were also reported in the Family Mediation Pilot Project report (Ellis, 1994).[4] In this longitudinal study, clients of lawyers and mediators were asked how satisfied they were with their lawyers and mediators. Their answers were located on a 5-point scale, ranging from *very satisfied* to *very dissatisfied*. Almost three quarters (73%) of female lawyer clients reported being very satisfied or satisfied and 16% reported being very dissatisfied or dissatisfied. Among females in the mediation sample, only 53.4% reported being very satisfied or satisfied and 28.0% reported being very dissatisfied or dissatisfied with their lawyers. The difference in satisfaction-dissatisfaction with lawyers reported by clients of lawyers and mediators is statistically significant ($p < .05$). Compared with mediation clients, then, a significantly higher proportion of lawyer clients reported being satisfied with their lawyers.

The proportion of lawyer clients who reported being satisfied with their lawyers is not significantly different from the proportion of mediation clients who reported being satisfied with their mediators (73% vs. 64%).

Turning from persons to process, clients in the two samples were asked about participating in the same dispute resolution process if they were starting the separation process all over again. A preponderance (81%) of female lawyer clients said they would. The comparable figure for female mediation clients is 64.3%. When they were asked whether they would recommend lawyer negotiations or mediation to a friend who was separating, 78.7% of female lawyer clients said they would recommend lawyer negotiations and 64.3% of female mediation clients said they would recommend mediation. The percentage difference in the answers to both questions by female clients in the two samples is statistically significant ($p < .05$).

Among males in the mediation sample, a higher proportion would participate in mediation than in lawyer negotiations again (73.4% vs. 57.1%). This difference is statistically significant ($p < .05$). The relatively small number of males in the lawyer client sample ($n = 25$) undermines the stability of findings based on quantitative (percentage) comparisons.

Analysis of qualitative data revealed that males in the lawyer sample were the least satisfied group. The award of sole custody to their wives and "having to make [child support] payments I can't afford" were significant sources of dissatisfaction. Far fewer males in the mediation sample expressed dissatisfaction with these outcomes. Where sole custody was awarded to wives, liberal access arrangements were also likely to be arranged. Where joint custody was agreed on, male satisfaction levels were even higher.

In interpreting these findings, a number of considerations are relevant. First, higher levels of satisfaction reported by female clients in the lawyer sample with respect to custody are partly a function of the fact that this issue was easier for lawyers to settle because the requests for sole custody by the wives in this sample were not challenged by husbands. The request for joint custody by a higher proportion of husbands in the mediation sample made the issue of custody more difficult to settle in a mutually satisfying way.[5] Lawyer effectiveness in settling the issues of custody could account for higher levels of satisfaction by female lawyer clients.

Second, because of differences in the sex composition of the mediation and lawyer client samples, we could not use a joint measure of satisfaction based on the responses of both husbands and wives. Instead, we only measured levels of satisfaction reported by wives in the two samples. The mediation process emphasizes compromise and joint or collective (family) outcomes. The lawyer negotiation process places relatively greater emphasis on winning and on individual outcomes. For this reason, wives in the lawyer sample are more likely to see themselves as "winners," or to be persuaded that they are. "Winners" are probably more likely than "compromisers" to express satisfaction with the process and the professionals who helped them win.

Third, lawyer interventions were implicated in the mediation process. In some cases, lawyers were involved as comediators. In all of them, lawyers gave advice relating to the issues in contention and reviewed the agreement. A relatively high proportion of mediation clients were dissatisfied with their lawyers. This may have contributed to a decrease in their satisfaction with the mediation process. This interpretation is supported by the findings of Ogus et al. (1989). They found that dissatisfaction with mediation increased with the participation of lawyers in the process.

The researchers whose work has been cited here also provided information on reasons for the higher level of client satisfaction among male and female mediation participants. These included the following responses: "mediator helped me stand up for my rights" (71%), "was fair" (82%), "provided enough information to protect my interests" (75%), "mediator showed concern for my feelings" (75%), "spousal support was fair" (66%), and "custody and visitation arrangements were best for everyone" (66%; Kelly and Gigy, 1989, p. 279). The only significant sex difference reported by Kelly and Gigy had to do with child support: 37% of the women but only 3% of the men agreed that child support payments were inadequate.

Pearson and Thoennes (1989) reported these responses: Mediation "helped me focus on the needs of the children" (69%), "gave me a chance to express my own point of view" (70% to 90%), and "was less rushed and superficial [than the court process]" (72%) (pp. 19-20). Reasons for a lower level of satisfaction with the court process include "unfair custody investigations," treating private matters in public, and participant lack of control over the process (p. 20).

Emery and Wyer (1987b) make an important contribution to understanding gender variations in satisfaction by placing mediation and litigation in a legal context. Although the standard of "best interest of the child" is the regnant legal rule, the "tender years" standard it replaced still exerts an influence on the decisions of judges. As a result, most female parents who go to court are granted sole custody in the belief that this is in the best interest of the children. Mothers who participate in mediation are participating in a dispute resolution process in which the risk of not obtaining sole custody is greater than it would have been had they gone to court. Fathers, who are frequently losers in court contests for custody, improve their chances of obtaining the kind of custody arrangements they want by participating in mediation. Hence, the best interests of the child is more likely to be associated with joint custody. Different comparison levels for alternatives (Thibaut &

Kelly, 1965) are reflected in gender differences in satisfaction among participants in custody or visitation mediation.

Taken together, the evidence presented here supports the hypothesis that client satisfaction varies across mediation and adversarial client groups, with clients in the former group reporting higher levels of satisfaction than clients in the latter group. The reasons for higher or different levels of satisfaction cover both process and outcomes. Unfortunately, the effects of process and outcomes on client satisfaction were confounded in the research studies we reviewed. In the studies we report on next, explicit attempts were made to assess the independent effects of process and outcomes on client satisfaction.

Process, Outcomes, and Satisfaction

In their study of conciliation (mediation) in England and Wales, Ogus (1991) and Ogus et al. (1989) compared agreement and satisfaction rates across four types of mediation service. The primary criterion used in classifying these services was the "predominant form of institutional control of the mediation service" (Ogus et al., 1989, p. 71). The application of this criterion assisted in classifying the mediation service as either court-based or independent of the court. A second criterion was "the degree of control or influence exerted by the judicial process" (p. 71). The application of this criterion yielded court-based services with high and low judicial control. Independent (non-court-based) mediation services in England and Wales may vary in the degree to which they are controlled or influenced by the probation service via the provision of premises, funding, administration, and mediators. Applying this external authority criterion yielded two types of independent mediation services, those with and those without (or with very little) probation control.

On the basis of these criteria, the following four types of custody or access mediation services were selected for study:

Court A: Court-based mediation with high judicial control (4 services)
Court B: Court-based mediation with low judicial control (2 services)
Court C: Independent mediation with probation control (3 services)
Court D: Independent mediation with no probation control (4 services)

Agreement and client satisfaction rates for these four types of mediation service are presented in Table 8.1.

This table shows that the satisfaction rate is higher than the agreement rate for the two independent mediation services (C and D) and lower than the agreement rate for the two court-based services (A and B). The direction and size of the difference between the agreement and satisfaction rates indicate that client satisfaction varies inversely with the presence of external legal or other authoritative influence on the mediation service. In other words, client satisfaction is lowest in the court with high judicial control (A) and highest among clients of non-court-based mediation services with no external control by probation services.

This finding suggests that the association between process, agreements, and satisfaction is mediated by the legal context in which mediation takes place. Mediation services that are relatively independent of formal legal authorities (judges and probation office) produce higher levels of satisfaction among clients than court-based mediation services with a high degree of judicial control.

Judicial control over the mediation process may also have varied across the two mediation service models (open vs. closed) studied by Depner et al. (1994). Mediator power potential and persuasive strength were almost certainly greater in the open model. In the open model, but not in the closed one, mediators were authorized to make recommendations to the court for custody and access/visitation where parents had reached an impasse. However, no significant differences were found in general satisfaction, helpfulness, and opportunity to discuss issues between open and closed mediation.

In the Family Mediation Pilot Project (Ellis, 1994), clients participating in a comprehensive court-based mediation service with low judicial control were compared with clients of lawyers in private practice who were paid out of public funds (Legal Aid). Table 8.2 shows how settlement and satisfaction rates varied by membership in these two groups.

The first column in this table shows the number of clients who brought the issue in question to mediation or lawyer negotiations. Thus, 37 (47.4%) of the female mediation clients and 65 (63.7%) of the female lawyer clients brought the issue of child support for settlement. The second column shows the percentage of these clients who reported having settled the issue.[6] For example, 24.3% of mediation clients (37)

Table 8.1 Agreement and Satisfaction Rates Reported by Four Mediation Services, by Percentage

Court	Agreement Rate for Custody and Access	Satisfaction Rate Regarding Process	Score Difference
A	39	28	−11
B	61	57	−4
C	64	70	+6
D	41	67	+26

SOURCE: Adapted from Ogus (1991, p. 18).
NOTE: The figures in this table are approximations because the figures included in the Ogus report are small and difficult to read.

and 63.7% of lawyer clients (65) fell into this category. The next column shows the percentage of clients who are satisfied with the settlement of the issue. The base figure is the number of clients bringing the issue to the mediators or lawyers for settlement. Thus, 43.8% of 37 female mediation clients and 41.7% of 65 female lawyer clients reported being satisfied with the settlement of the issue of child support. Note that the base for both settlement and satisfaction percentages is the same.

Table 8.2 also shows differences between settlement rates and satisfaction rates among females in the mediation and lawyer samples. Two findings are noteworthy: First, for each of the four issues included in Table 8.2, female lawyer clients reported significantly higher settlement rates. Thus, 83.1% of them reported settlement of the issue of child support as compared with 24.3% of female mediation clients. The percentage differences for the other three issues are almost as great.

Second, among female mediation clients, the proportion of satisfied clients is greater than the proportion reporting the settlement of issues. Among female lawyer clients, the proportion of satisfied clients is smaller than the proportion reporting the settlement of issues. Thus, 24.3% of 37 female mediation clients reported settlement of the child support issue, but 43.8% of them reported being satisfied with mediation as a method of settling conflicts associated with this issue. Clearly, satisfied mediation clients include some females for whom the issue of child support was not settled. On the other hand, 83.1% of 65 female

Table 8.2 Issues in Contention, Settlement Rates, and Satisfaction with Settlements for Females: Comparison of Mediation and Lawyer Samples

	Mediation (n = 77)				Lawyer (n = 102)			
	Clients		Settlement Rate[b]	Satisfied Clients[c]	Clients		Settlement Rate	Satisfied Clients
Issues[a]	Number	Percentage[d]	Percentage	Percentage	Number	Percentage	Percentage	Percentage
Child support	37	47.4	24.3	43.8	65	63.7	83.1	41.7
Custody	31	39.7	32.3	40.0	30	29.4	80.0	96.4
Access	54	69.2	52.8	60.0	53	52.0	83.0	63.8
Property division	28	27.4	25.0	41.6	40	39.2	77.5	59.4

a. Figures reflect responses to the question, "Which of the following issues did you bring to mediation or lawyer negotiations?" Spousal support is not included in this table because there were too few cases.
b. Figures reflect responses to the question, "Did your lawyer or mediator help you settle all, some, or none of the issues you brought to them for settlement?"
c. Figures reflect responses to the question, "How satisfied are you with what the process of mediation or lawyer negotiations did for you with respect to the issues you wanted settled?"
d. Figures refer to the percentage of females in the mediation and lawyer samples who brought one or more of the four issues listed to mediation or lawyer negotiations for settlement.

lawyer clients reported settlement of the issue of child support, but a significantly smaller proportion, 41.7%, reported being satisfied with lawyer negotiations as a method of solving child support conflicts. Equally clearly, a significant proportion of lawyer clients who reported the settlement of this issue are not satisfied with the process that brought it about.

The difference between settlement and satisfaction described for the issues of child support also applies to the issues of custody, access, and property division. For all four issues, the proportion of satisfied mediation clients is greater than the proportion reporting settlements. Among female lawyer clients, the same situation obtains only with respect to the issue of custody.

In interpreting these findings, it is important to note that the differences between settlement and satisfaction rates among lawyer clients may be partly due to the time and cost constraints under which the lawyers worked. Legal Aid provides publicly funded loans to persons who cannot afford to retain a lawyer without them. For "legal aid lawyers," the tariff is relatively low—between 40% and 60% of the hourly rate they would charge clients if they were retained privately.[7] Limiting the amount of work they put into a case to what is covered by the legal aid fee schedule tends to speed up the settlement process. A "no frills" or "few frills" lawyer negotiation process is likely to produce speedier settlements than an "all the frills" one in which the parties have the resources to pay for them.

A few-frills lawyer negotiation process appears to be one in which relatively little time is taken to communicate with clients. Qualitative data indicate that lack of communication about their cases was a major source of irritation among lawyer clients.

Summary of Findings

Mediated agreement rates range from 40% to 80%, with an average rate of approximately 60%.

Mediated agreement rates vary with timing, with the rates being higher among those who commence mediation prior to becoming involved with formal legal procedures (e.g., filing an application, contacting a lawyer, completing an affidavit).

Client satisfaction varies positively with reaching an agreement, but the strength of the association is attenuated by the fact that a significant, albeit smaller, proportion of clients are satisfied even though they did not reach agreements.

Client satisfaction does not vary with participation in open or closed mediation.

Client satisfaction does not vary with participation in voluntary or mandatory mediation.

Client satisfaction varies with participation in mediation or adversarial processes, with satisfaction being higher among mediation clients.

Client satisfaction varies with custody or access (visitation) or litigation varies with gender, with mediation fathers being equally or more satisfied than mediation mothers and litigation mothers being more satisfied than litigation fathers.

Client satisfaction with the process of mediation varies inversely with judicial or lawyer control or involvement, with clients participating in

non-court-based service with low judicial or lawyer control or involvement reporting higher levels of satisfaction.

Among mediation clients, satisfaction rates are higher than settlement rates
for child support, custody, access, and property division

Among lawyer clients, satisfaction rates are lower than settlement rates for
child support, access, and property division and higher for custody.

Conclusions

▓ Mothers who value sole custody above all other outcomes are far more
likely to achieve this outcome through lawyer negotiations, court hearings,
or trials and are therefore more likely than fathers to be satisfied with these
adversarial processes.

▓ Fathers who value joint physical custody, joint legal custody, or sole
custody with liberal access arrangements are more likely to achieve these
outcomes through mediation and are therefore more likely than mothers
to be satisfied with this process.

▓ The control or involvement of judges and lawyers in the mediation process
decreases the level of client satisfaction with this process.

▓ The setting in which mediation takes place (inside a court or in a separate
building) influences the level of client satisfaction.

▓ Clients participating in open mediation or mandatory mediation are as
satisfied as those participating in closed or voluntary mediation.

▓ With outcomes valued by clients held constant, mediation clients are more
satisfied with mediation than adversarial clients are with the processes of
lawyer negotiation, court hearings, and trials.

Notes

1. For an opposing view, see Grillo (1991).

2. Litigation participants were paid more than mediation participants, but Emery and
Wyer (1987b) state that this did not influence the findings.

3. Some participants were interviewed 1 week later, and others were interviewed less
than 5 weeks later. This relatively brief postprocessing period raises questions about the
stability of their findings.

4. In this study, postprocessing interviews were held 12 months later.

5. Of the 25 men in the lawyer sample, 15 answered the relevant question and none of
them wanted joint custody. The comparable figure for men in the mediation sample is 21
of 57 (36.8%).

6. Settlement covers both mediation agreements and lawyer memoranda of understanding. A single term is being used to facilitate exposition.

7. The standard hourly rate for the lawyer with an average amount of experience is $67.00 per hour. Highly experienced lawyers receive $85.00 per hour. Additional payments are made for disbursements and preparation time. Hourly fees for lawyers in private practice in Hamilton and St. Catharines range from $125.00 to $260.00 per hour. The mean or average hourly fee is $149.00 per hour.

9

Compliance

The concept of compliance focuses attention on the postseparation-postdivorce conduct of ex-partners. More specifically, we shall use compliance to refer to compliance with mediated agreements, lawyer-negotiated memoranda of understandings, and judicial determinations (i.e., court orders). Compliance is usually measured by examining court records (relitigation rates), by interviewing ex-spouses (self-report compliance rates), or both.

In evaluating compliance rates, a few points ought to be kept in mind. First and foremost, compliance rates may be influenced by a variety of factors *other than* the type of the original dispute-ending process. Thus, compliance with custody and access arrangements may change markedly following relocation due to a job change, remarriage, or illness regardless of whether mediated agreements, memoranda of understandings, or judicial orders ended their original issue-related conflicts.

Second, in evaluating the effects of mediation, lawyer negotiations, court orders, or relitigation rates, it is necessary to separate the contribution made to these rates by contempt motions, unilateral motions, and collaborative motions.[1] *Contempt motions* have to do with the enforcement of court orders. *Unilateral motions* have to do with requests to the court by one party to vary or change orders (e.g., a mother asking for increased child support because she has discovered that her ex-husband has been given a job promotion with an increase in salary). *Collaborative motions* are requests to the court by both partners to vary or change orders (e.g., both parents ask that their eldest son change his residence from the home of one to the home of the other). Clearly, a process that increases the ratio of collaborative to contempt and unilateral motions is not increasing the noncompliance rate, even though its overall relitigation rate may be higher than that produced by other marital dispute resolution processes.

Compliance: Court-Recorded (Relitigation) Rates

Relitigation, or more specifically, "patterns of relitigation," was the focus of a study published by Koel, Clark, Straus, Whitney, and Houser (1994). Their sample consisted of 1,400 court records of divorced couples. Of these, 700 couples had children and 700 did not. The authors believe that litigation and relitigation are associated with "poor outcomes for [divorced] parents and their children, and [are] therefore a cause for concern" (p. 265). Their primary objective was to document the effects of relitigation on postdivorce families.

The time period during which relitigation motions were filed varied between 38 months and 125 months after divorce, with an average of 87 months. One of the best predictors of relitigation during this period was found to be the presence of children. They found that "41% of the 700 couples with children (287 families) but only 6.6% of the 700 couples without children (46 families) relitigated" (p. 269). This difference is statistically significant. Parents who returned to court filed an average of 4.3 motions (range 1 to 28), whereas ex-spouses without children filed an average of 2.6 (range 1 to 13 motions). This difference is also statistically significant.

In their discussion of the effect of litigation on the quality of postdivorce family life, Ann Koel et al. (1994) imply that alternative dispute resolution processes may have more benign, or at least less malign, effects because of the effect of interparental conflict on choice of marital dispute resolution process. They hypothesize that high-conflict parents tend to choose litigation, whereas low-conflict parents tend to choose nonadversarial processes, such as mediation. High interparental conflict is associated with litigation, and litigation, they contend, is associated with relitigation involving a high proportion of contempt and contested unilateral motions.

Evidence in support of these hypotheses is not presented because they did not include mediation families in their sample. Joan Kelly (1990a) did include mediation and adversarial families in her sample, but because of problems with data entry and sample attrition, she did not report separate relitigation rates for families in these two groups. Instead, she combined them and reports that 12 months after the final divorce, "fifteen percent of all respondents indicated that they had seen an attorney or gone to court to change or enforce the terms of their divorce agreement" (p. 22). The 12-month (and 2-year) relitigation rate for parents with children was 20%. This difference (15% vs. 20%) is not significant. Unlike Koel and her associates, Kelly did not find the presence of children to be a statistically significant predictor of relitigation rates. Moreover, the rate reported by Koel is more than twice as high as the rate reported by Kelly (41% vs. 20%).

The presence of mediation families in the Kelly sample may have markedly muted or attenuated the relitigation rate. This is one probable reason for differences in the relitigation rates reported by Kelly and Koel.[2] Empirical evidence supporting it is provided by Pearson and Thoennes (1989). In their Denver study, they found that 13% of mediation clients and 35% of adversarial clients returned to court to file contempt, unilateral, and collaborative motions during a 2-year postdivorce period. This difference is statistically significant. In a later three-state study (Divorce Mediation Research Project), however, Pearson and Thoennes (1988) found that 21% of successful mediation clients, 31% of unsuccessful mediation clients, and 36% of adversarial clients returned to court "to file contempt charges, to take out temporary restraining orders, or to modify custody, visitation or child support" during an approximately 1-year postprocessing period (p. 12). The difference between successful mediation clients and adversarial clients is significant (21% vs. 36%), but the difference between unsuccessful mediation clients and adversarial clients is not (31% vs. 36%). Relitigation rates for participants in these two processes were very similar 5 years after they had participated in mediation or the adversary process (25%).

Based on findings derived from the study of court-based (custody and visitation) mediation in four states and involving interviews with 667 mediation clients and 189 adversarial clients, Pearson and Thoennes reached the following modest conclusion: "While mediation may not always be more effective than adjudication in preventing relitigation . . . [m]ediated agreements are no less stable than those originating from court orders or lawyer conducted negotiations" (p. 22). Support for this conclusion is also provided by Kressel and Pruitt (1989). They reviewed the relevant literature and found that "in no study are the data on relitigation rates *less* favorable with mediation" (p. 396).

This finding stands without prejudice to the Kelly (1990b) finding that mediation clients report lower relitigation rates than adversarial clients during the first year or two following mediation. Is a higher level of interparental conflict at least partly responsible for this difference, as Koel et al. (1994) suggest? The answer to this question is "probably not," because, in the Kelly study, the levels of conflict in the mediation and adversarial groups were similar prior to their participation in mediation or the adversarial process. Kelly (1990b) states, "The adversarial and mediation groups did not differ at the beginning of divorce in the . . . reported level of marital conflict, child-specific conflict" (p. 9).

Another possible reason for this difference is suggested by the findings of Ellis (1994). Like Kelly, Ellis found similar baseline or preprocessing levels of conflict among mediation and adversarial parents who reported different levels of compliance problems. A constant, such as similar levels of conflict, cannot explain or account for a variable, such as compliance problems. However, recency of abuse (i.e., wife abuse occurring during the 6 months prior to separation) did vary between these groups and was found to be a statistically significant predictor of compliance problems reported by female mediation parents but not female adversarial parents. This finding suggests that recency of wife abuse, not conflict, is associated with compliance problems among female mediation clients. The interaction between recency of abuse and joint custody arrangements may help account for this finding.[3]

Compliance: Self-Reported Rates

Findings from the Denver Custody Mediation Project (Pearson & Thoennes, 1984) indicate that compliance rates vary with participation in mediation or the adversarial process, with the rate being significantly higher for participants in the mediation process. Of the clients with mediated agreements, 80% reported that their partners had complied with all terms of the agreement. The comparable figure for clients in the adversarial group was 60%. This is a significant difference (Pearson & Thoennes, 1984). Findings from the Divorce Mediation Research Project (Pearson & Thoennes, 1989) indicate that among parents who were receiving child support and who successfully completed mediation, one third reported irregular or absent payments. The comparable figure for clients whose custody arrangements were adjudicated is one half. With respect to access, none of the noncustodial parents in the mediation group reported infrequent visits with their children, but 30% of those in the adversarial group reported that they "rarely saw their children" (p. 21). Similar findings are reported by Kelly (1990b), and on the basis of her findings, she concluded that "mediation respondents are more in compliance with final divorce arrangements than adversarial respondents" (p. 20).

This sanguine conclusion may not apply when mandatory, "one shot mediation" is compared with the adversarial process. Thus, Pearson and Thoennes (1984) found that approximately the same proportion of clients in the mediation and adversarial groups reported that their spouses had failed to comply with the terms of their agreements (p. 22). Pearson and Thoennes explain this finding in these terms: "Although it [i.e., one brief court-based, mandatory, child-support-focused mediation session] was an informal process, it lacked many of the communicative, therapeutic and bargaining features usually associated with mediation" (p. 20). The effect of mediation on postprocessing rates of wife abuse also varies with regular or "one-time" mediation. Ellis and Stuckless (1992) found that wives participating in one mandatory or coerced mediation session reported significantly higher wife abuse rates than those participating in six to eight 1-hour court-based mediation sessions over a period of 2 or 3 months.

Compliance problems also appear to vary with the type of mediation service. Ogus et al. (1989) compared compliance rates for court-based and independent mediation services; they found compliance rates to be somewhat higher among the latter. Specifically, they found that 50% of independent mediation clients and 44% of court-based mediation clients reported never having had problems relating to their partner's compliance with the terms of their mediated agreements, whereas 35% of clients in the latter group ($n = 67$) and 28% of clients in the former group ($n = 86$) reported experiencing problems "during the first year after they had reached an agreement" (p. 274).[4]

In his family mediation pilot project, Ellis (1994) provides evidence indicating that compliance problems also vary with the issues and the sex of clients. Table 9.1 shows that problems with child support were reported by more than one third, problems with access by more than one quarter, and problems with custody and property division by fewer than one fifth of the 263 clients in the comparison sample.

Problems with child support and access were also reported by the highest proportion of females in the mediation and lawyer samples. When these were compared, a significant difference in the proportions reporting problems with access was revealed, as shown in Table 9.1: 39.7% of female mediator clients and 18.9% of female lawyer clients reported problems with agreed-on access arrangements. Differences in the proportions reporting problems with child support, access, and property division are relatively small.

In interpreting the finding of a significant difference in compliance with agreed-on access arrangements, two considerations are relevant. First, disagreements over access arrangements were more serious for female mediation clients when compared with female lawyer clients. They had spent twice as many months as female lawyer clients (12 months vs. 6 months) attempting to settle arrangements prior to commencing mediation and lawyer negotiations, respectively. In addition, between one quarter and one third of female mediation clients had come to mediation after the lawyers they had retained failed to negotiate a satisfactory settlement of the interrelated issues of child custody, access, and support. Second, it is possible that more frequent contacts and more flexible access arrangements agreed to by mediation clients are associ-

Table 9.1 Percentages of Postprocessing Problems in Complying With Agreements and Minutes of Settlement, by Sample and Sex

	Comparison	Females		Mediation		Comparison[a]	
Problems	All (n = 263)	Mediation (n = 77)	Lawyer (n = 102)	Males (n = 57)	Females (n = 77)	Males (n = 82)	Females (n = 179)
Child support	34.6	42.3	33.3	33.3	42.3	29.3	37.4
Custody	19.2	18.5	6.9	37.5	18.5	31.9	13.2
Access	28.0	39.7	18.9	31.3	29.7	28.4	28.0
Property division	10.3	1.3	8.3	8.3	15.4	9.8	10.6

NOTE: Figures refer to yes answers to the following questions: "Have you had problems with receiving or paying the agreed-on amount of child support regularly and on time?" and "Have the custody or access arrangements worked out as agreed on?"
a. Males and females in the comparison sample do not sum to 263 because the sex of two respondents was not recorded.

ated with more problems during the first few months they are in place. These may take more than a few months to solve.[5]

Compared with females in the mediation sample, a significantly higher proportion of males in the same sample report compliance problems with respect to custody agreements. Specifically, 37.5% of males and 18.5% of females report custody compliance problems. Male-female client differences in the proportions reporting problems with the issues of child support, access, and property division are relatively small.

To some mediation clients, their mediators and lawyers are perceived as "urging" joint physical custody. This agreement does appear to cause additional friction, at least during the initial months of implementation. One representative comment is this one:

> Joint custody may be good for children, but mediators and lawyers really push it. . . . Our children go from one house to another every 2 or 3 days . . . they're always on the move. It's hard on me and hard on my ex.

Not infrequently, any observable change in the ex-partner's lifestyle and personal relations (new girlfriend or boyfriend sleeps over, new carpets installed, etc.) are reported back (usually innocently) to the parents by the children, and these reports set off a new round of conflicts or continue old ones. The more frequently the children move from one parent to the other, the more this is likely to happen.

When males and females in the comparison sample were compared, significantly higher proportions of males reported problems with respect to the issue of custody (31.9% vs. 13.2%), as Table 9.1 shows. Differences in the proportions reporting compliance problems with respect to the issues of child support, access, and property division are relatively small, and their patterning does not consistently favor either males or females.

Problems associated with failures to comply with agreements and settlements may result in further legal action. One possibility in Canada is recourse to the Family Support Plan (FSP), Ministry of the Attorney General. Approximately 40% of all clients in the comparison sample did not report failure to comply with agreed-on child support payment agreements to FSP. The comparable figures for the female mediation and lawyer clients who reported becoming involved with FSP were 40% and 48%, respectively. Among mediation clients, the proportions of male and female clients who reported becoming involved with FSP were 30% and 40%, respectively. The comparable figures for male and female clients in the comparison sample were 28% and 45%, respectively. This difference is significant.

Another specific measure of compliance with agreements and settlements is the proportion of clients who reported having to see a lawyer again, having to return to court to settle alleged noncompliance with agreed-on arrangements, or both. For all four issues combined (child support, custody, access, and property division), the proportion of female mediation and lawyer clients who reported returning to court was approximately equal (10.8% and 10.1%). Among female lawyer clients who returned to court, the highest proportion did so to settle noncompliance with child support payments (22.5%). Among female mediation clients who returned to court, the highest proportion did so to settle the issues of child support (15.6%) and access (15.6%).

Compared with those who returned to court, a slightly higher proportion of female clients in the mediation and lawyer samples reported having to see a lawyer again. Specifically, for all four issues combined, 17.9% of the former and 15.0% of the latter reported doing this. Among these female lawyer clients, the highest proportion (28.4%) saw a lawyer again because of problems with child support payments. Among female mediation clients who saw lawyers again, the highest proportion did so to settle problems with child support payments (24.7%) and access (24.7%). None of these difference reported here are statistically significant. When all the indicators identified are included in a compliance scale, differences in noncompliance reported by female lawyer and mediation clients are not statistically significant.

In an attempt to identify variables that were strongly associated with compliance, correlation analysis was done. An examination of the correlation matrix (Ellis, 1994) revealed that seven variables were significantly associated with partner compliance among female mediation clients. These are (a) satisfaction with lawyer, (b) negotiation outcomes, (c) seriousness of disagreements, (d) postprocessing abuse, (e) alcohol or drug problems, (f) wanted-got child support, and (g) wanted-got custody. Two of the variables are preprocessing variables (seriousness of disagreements and alcohol or drug problems). One of them refers to the mediator (satisfaction) and three refer to the outcomes of mediation (negotiation outcomes, wanted-got child support, and wanted-got custody). The one remaining postprocessing variable is postprocessing abuse. Three of the seven were also significantly associated with compliance among clients in the lawyer sample. These are (a) satisfaction with lawyer, (b) seriousness of disagreements, and (c) postprocessing abuse. Harassment is significantly associated with compliance in this sample but not in the mediation sample.

Last, we turn our attention to the task of predicting postprocessing compliance with arrangements set out in mediation agreements and lawyer-negotiated settlements. The same nine predictors were initially entered into the two predictive models (Ellis, 1994). These are (a) expecting to have to go to court to settle the issues of property division or access, (b) satisfaction with lawyer or mediator, (c) income, (d) partner's use of alcohol or drugs, (e) education, (f) seriousness of disagreements, (g) economic condition, (h) abuse during the 6 months prior to separation, and (i) postprocessing abuse. Stepwise regression procedures eliminated nonsignificant variables, reducing the number of variables to three in the female mediation model (seriousness of disagreements, abuse during the 6 months prior to separation, and postprocessing abuse), and to five in the female lawyer model. These five included the three entered in the mediation model plus preprocessing expectations about having to go to court to have the issues of child support or property division settled.

The three variables entered in the female mediation model explained 39% of the total variation in compliance ($R^2 = 39\%$). The model was statistically significant ($p<.01$). The two abuse variables, recency of abuse and postprocessing abuse, were both statistically significant: seriousness of disagreements was not. The preprocessing variable (abuse during the 6 months prior to separation) explained 34.8% of the total variation (i.e., 39%).

The five variables entered in the female lawyer model explained 49% of the total variation in compliance. The model was also statistically significant ($p<.05$). Preprocessing expectations about having to go to court to have an issue of child support settled explained 20% of the total variation (i.e., 49%; Ellis, 1994).

Two preprocessing predictors of compliance were included in both the female mediation and the female lawyer models. These are (a) seriousness of disagreements prior to commencing mediation or lawyer negotiations and (b) abuse during the 6 months prior to separation. The two models differed from each other in the following ways: The preprocessing variable, abuse during the 6 months prior to separation, and postprocessing abuse were statistically significant predictors in the female mediation client model. A preprocessing variable, expecting to have to go to court to settle the custody issue, was the only statistically significant predictor in the female lawyer client model.

Summary of Findings

Relitigation rates vary with the presence of children and the composition of study samples, with parents with children reporting higher rates in litigation-only samples and parents with and without children reporting similar rates in blended (mediation and adversarial client) samples.

Relitigation rates vary with (a) participation in mediation or the adversarial process and (b) time, with adversarial clients reporting higher rates during the 1st or 2nd postdivorce year and clients in both groups reporting similar rates by the end of 5 years after divorce.

Compliance problems vary with participation in mediation or the adversarial process, with mediation clients reporting higher levels of compliance with the terms of the agreements by their ex-partners.

Compared with clients participating in regular mediation (multiple sessions over 2 or 3 months), those participating in mandatory, one-time mediation report lower levels of compliance with the terms of their agreements.

Compliance problems vary with the issues in contention, with custody or access problems or both being reported by the highest proportion of clients in the combined mediation and adversarial sample.

Compliance problems vary with the marital dispute resolution process and the issue in contention, with twice as many female mediation clients than female lawyer clients reporting compliance problems with access arrangements.

Compliance problems vary with gender, with a significantly higher proportion of male clients reporting access problems and a significantly higher proportion of female clients reporting child support problems.

Wife abuse during the 6 months prior to separation is a statistically significant predictor of compliance problems reported by female mediation clients.

Expecting to have to go to court to have the issue of child custody settled is a statistically significant predictor of compliance problems reported by female lawyer clients.

Conclusions

■ Lawyer negotiations and mediation are equally effective in preventing ex-partners from returning to court to settle compliance problems with custody, access, support, or property division arrangements.

■ Mediation is more effective than lawyer negotiations in preventing noncompliance with agreed-on custody and support arrangements, but not access arrangements, during the 1st postagreement year.

■ Factors beyond the control of mediators and lawyers, such as preprocessing abuse and seriousness of disagreements over issues, are partly responsible for partner noncompliance problems.

■ Relatively brief marital conflict resolution processes, such as mediation, lawyer negotiations, hearings, and trials, are relatively ineffective in changing mutually harmful relationships established over a number of years into stable, cooperative, mutually helpful postdivorce relationships.

Notes

1. See Koel et al. (1994).

2. Other possible reasons include differences in the way relitigation rates were defined, the time at which they were measured, and the way they were measured. Koel et al. (1994) operationally defined the relitigation rate as postdivorce "requests for action by the court," that is, postdivorce contempt and modification motions (p. 268). Kelly (1990b) operationally defined the same rate as postdivorce reports by clients who reported they had "seen an attorney or gone to court to change or enforce the terms of their divorce agreement" (p. 22). Because Kelly's definition is broader in that it includes seeing an attorney, her measures should have yielded a higher relitigation rate, but they did not. Next, Kelly's measures were taken at 1 and 2 years after the final divorce had been granted, whereas Koel and her associates measured relitigation rates at an average of 7 years and 3 months after divorce. Last, Koel et al.'s measures were entries in court records (motions), whereas Kelly's measures were self-reported by clients who were interviewed.

3. Other factors that could also account for this finding have been cited by Kressel and Pruitt (1989, pp. 396-397).

4. The number of postagreement years during which mediation clients report never having had problems is not clear from the contents of their report.

5. For evidence supporting this interpretation, see Kitzmann (1993).

Economic Consequences

In 1985, Lenore Weitzman published the results of her study on the social and economic consequences of divorce in the United States. One of her more general findings was that husbands earned more than their wives prior to the divorce and that the differences in their incomes were even greater 1 year following their divorces. This finding led Weitzman to conclude that income inequality between husbands and wives is exacerbated by marital conflict resolution processes that operate under the shadow of no-fault divorce laws.[1]

It is possible for different marital conflict resolution processes working under the same legal shadow to be associated with negligible or large differences in the postdivorce family incomes of husbands and wives. Unfortunately, Weitzman did not report findings on postdivorce incomes for husbands and wives who participated in mediation or the adversarial process. Jessica Pearson (1991) did, however.

Pearson conducted telephone interviews with 302 divorced persons, 40% of whom settled matters between themselves. The remainder settled some issues by participating in mediation and other issues through lawyer negotiations or judicial intervention. Interview data yielded the following findings.[2]

First, at 3 years postdivorce, women who reached agreements on financial issues through mediation reported earning a higher percentage of their incomes at separation than women who settled these issues on their own or through the adversarial process. The figures are 56% (mediation), 49% (on their own), and 43% (adversarial). This translates into annual postseparation incomes of $29,274 (mediation), $26,415 (on their own), and $21,490 (adversarial). Separated women in the mediation group, then, not only earn a higher proportion of their preseparation incomes but also higher annual salaries than women in the "on our own" and adversarial groups.

The differences in annual postseparation income levels could reflect similar differences in income levels at separation. This possibility is suggested by the fact that 56% of the women in the mediation group had college degrees, compared with 36% of those in the "on our own" group and 33% in the adversarial group. Based on these findings, Pearson (1991) reaches the following conclusion: "Economic disparities between men and women following divorce reflect differences in earning capacity that cannot be easily addressed through the selection of a forum in which divorce agreements are generated" (p. 195).

Findings presented in her study suggest that the economic disparities she refers to are present *within* as well as *between* gender groups. At the same time, Pearson's conclusion underestimates the contribution made by choice of marital dispute resolution process to postseparation differences in the financial situation of separated women.

Her findings also indicate that joint physical custody arrangements vary with membership in different marital dispute resolution groups. This arrangement is reported to be in place by 30% of the women in the mediation group, 17% of those in the "on our own" group, and 8% in the adversarial (lawyer-judge) group. To the extent that joint physical custody equalizes child care and educational expenses incurred by fathers and mothers, a marital dispute resolution process that favors mediation is not as likely as the adversarial process to worsen the financial situations of separated women and may even make a greater contribution toward improving them. Conversely, a marital conflict resolution process that favors sole custody (adversarial process) exacerbates the financial problems of custodial parents.

The financial situation of separated women is also influenced by the level of compliance with orders, agreements, or understandings covering child and spousal support levels. In the Pearson (1991) study, compliance levels were found to be high, with members in the "on our own," mediation, and adversarial groups reporting equally high compliance rates. Differences in the average total amount of child support ordered were $362 (on our own), $442 (mediation), and $393 (adversarial). These payments represented 18%, 19%, and 21% of the net income of payers in the "on our own," mediation, and adversarial groups, respectively. On the basis of these findings, we conclude that absolute levels of child support, but not compliance rates, mediate the effects of marital dispute resolution processes on the financial situation of separated women. Mediation makes a slightly greater contribution toward improving the financial situation of separated women than private bilateral negotiation or the adversarial process via its effects on child support levels.

The award of spousal support to some wives but not others can also account for differences in the financial situation of separated women, but choice of marital conflict resolution process is relatively unimportant in accounting for it. This conclusion is based on the finding that husbands' incomes and duration of marriage virtually determine spousal support awards. Specifically, women who have been married for a long time to high-income earners are far more likely to be awarded spousal support than women who have been married less than 5 years to husbands earning under $33,000 annually (Pearson, 1991).[3]

Last, Pearson (1991) found that remarriage had a far greater effect on the financial situation of separated women than any other independent variable used in her study, including choice of marital conflict resolution process.[4] Females who remarried at some time during the 3 years following their separation reported that their average postseparation household income was 139% of their average household income at separation. The comparable figure for remarried males was 132%. Among unmarried females, the average postseparation household income was 49% of their average household income at separation. The comparable figure for unmarried males was 74%. Unmarried females, then, are far worse off economically than married females and males (Pearson, 1991).

In the Ellis (1994) study, approximately the same proportion (23%) of mediation and adversarial clients reported living with a new partner during their 1st postseparation year. During this period, almost half

(47.6%) of the total sample (mediation and adversarial clients) reported being in a "worse or much worse" economic condition. Approximately one third reported being in a "better or much better" economic condition. Table 10.1 shows that these postprocessing economic conditions are experienced unequally by males and females as well as by females in the lawyer and mediation samples; 27.9% more males than females reported being worse or much worse off economically and 26.8% more females than males reported being better or much better off economically. Compared with females in the mediation sample, 8.4% fewer females in the lawyer sample reported being worse or much worse off economically and 22.2% reported being better off. The differences between males and females in the comparison sample and between females in the lawyer and mediation samples are statistically significant (p < .05).

In interpreting the findings presented in this table, it is important to take into account preprocessing differences in economic circumstances. For example, compared with females in the mediation sample, 14% fewer females in the lawyer sample were employed and almost 20% fewer of them (19.5%) reported a gross monthly income of $2,000 or more. Females in the lawyer sample, then, were poorer to begin with—hence their application for a Legal Aid (Family) Certificate. As more of them were already living at subsidized societal safety net levels, their economic condition was already so bad it could only get better. Moreover, given their worse preprocessing economic condition, they were also more likely than mediation clients to report that quite small additions to their postprocessing incomes—say, $30.00 a month—made their economic condition better or much better than it had been. It is relevant to note that 49.0% of female lawyer clients were on welfare 12 months after the legal processing of their cases had been completed. The comparable figure for mediation clients was 28.6%.

Turning now to male-female client differences within the mediation sample, Table 10.2 shows that 27.3% more males than females reported being worse off and 20% of the females reported being better off economically following the processing of their separation.

Preprocessing differences in economic circumstances should be taken into account in interpreting these findings. Approximately 20% of females and 48% of males reported gross monthly preprocessing incomes of $2,000 or more, and 12% more of the males were employed.

Table 10.1 Self-Reported Economic Condition by Sample and Sex (by percentage)

Economic Condition	Comparison	Females		Comparison	
	Males and Females (n = 263)	Mediation (n = 77)	Lawyer (n = 102)	Males (n = 82)	Females (n = 179)
Much worse	23.0	14.7	15.8	40.5	15.3
Worse	24.6	29.3	19.8	26.6	23.9
No change	18.8	26.7	12.9	17.7	18.8
Better	21.1	21.3	29.7	10.1	26.1
Much better	12.5	8.0	21.8	5.1	15.9
Total	100.0	100.0	100.0	100.0	100.0

NOTE: Figures reflect answers to the question, "How would you describe your economic condition now as compared with before you separated?"

Table 10.2 Self-Reported Economic Condition by Sex: Mediation Sample (by percentage)

Economic Condition	Males (n = 57)	Females (n = 77)
Much worse	44.8	14.5
Worse	25.9	28.9
No change	19.0	26.3
Better	6.9	22.4
Much better	3.4	7.9
Total	100.0	100.0

NOTE: Figures reflect answers to the question, "How would you describe your economic condition now as compared with before you separated?"

Compared with females in the comparison sample, males were in a better economic condition than females. Thus, they would be more likely to make postprocessing income transfers to their females ex-partners and to report being worse off than before. Because a greater proportion of females was already at or near societal safety net levels of economic existence (102 or 60% of females were Legal Aid clients), even small increments to their postprocessing incomes were more likely to be reported as making their economic condition better. Here again, it is relevant to note that 38% of female clients but only 15% of male clients were on welfare 12 months following the legal processing of their separations.

Perusal of qualitative data included in the questionnaires suggests that getting jobs and receiving welfare payments and mothers' allowances are at least partly responsible for the difference in the reported improvement in economic circumstances by females in the lawyer client sample. Information on the contribution made by welfare payments is corroborated by qualitative data indicating that 49% of female lawyer clients but only 28.6% of female mediation clients reported being on welfare following the processing of their separation.

Summary of Findings

The financial situation of separated women varied with the marital conflict resolution process they participated in, with female mediation clients reporting a more favorable financial situation than female clients participating in the adversarial process.

The financial situation of separated women varied with their financial situation at separation, with women with higher incomes or the potential to earn higher incomes reporting higher postseparation incomes.

Custody arrangements and child support levels mediated the effects of mediation and the adversarial process on the financial situation of separated women.

Remarriage was one of the most significant influences on the financial situation of separated husbands and wives.

Compared with the choice of marital conflict resolution process, remarriage was a far more significant influence on the financial situation of separated husbands and wives.

Approximately half of the clients in the mediation and adversarial samples reported being worse or much worse off economically following the processing of their separations, and approximately one third reported being better off economically.

In absolute terms, males were better off economically than females prior to and following the processing of their separations.

Compared with females in the mediation sample, females in the lawyer sample reported a greater relative improvement in their economic condition following the processing of their separations.

Getting jobs and receiving welfare and mother's allowance payments are partly responsible for the difference in the reported improvement in economic circumstances by females in the lawyer client sample.

Conclusions

▓ The most significant determinants of the financial statuses of separated or divorced wives and husbands are situations that existed prior to participation in marital conflict resolution processes (e.g., income differences) and life events that follow such participation (e.g., remarriage).

▓ It is beyond the mandate or the capacity of marital conflict resolution processes to bring about income equality between separated or divorced husbands and wives by changing societal tax, day care, health, and employment equity policies.

Notes

1. A number of methodological problems undermine the validity of Weitzman's findings on the economic consequences of divorce. These should be taken into account in evaluating them. For example, standards of living vary with urban or rural residence, yet Weitzman used a standard of living index that, by her own account, does not appear to take residence into account. Another example is that financial statements are included in court records. She sampled 2,500 court dockets and interviewed 228 men and women in the Los Angeles area, yet no attempt was made to validate income and expenses data provided by interview subjects with the same data included in court dockets. Moreover, nothing she reports eliminates the possibility that wives were not the sole source of data on the incomes and family needs of husbands as well as their own incomes and family needs. Last, she does not validate the income and family needs data by comparing information provided by a subset of couples who may have been included in her sample nor did she select an interview sample with this possibility in mind. For a cautionary note on collecting financial data from separating spouses, see Pearson (1991). For a more general critique, see McIsaac (1986).

2. The mediation option includes mediation with lawyer review of the mediation agreement, and the adversarial option includes lawyer negotiations and judicial intervention. We cannot eliminate the possibility that some mediation clients had tried lawyer negotiations or that some adversarial clients had tried mediation.

3. See also McLindon (1987).

4. Weitzman (1985) discusses the economic consequences of remarriage for women but does not actually report relevant findings about the economic effects of remarriage on the ex-husbands and ex-wives in her interview sample. Her sample included 114 of the former and 114 of the latter.

Effects on Children

Children's adjustment to divorce has been found to vary in the incidence of prosocial conduct (e.g., cooperation, social support), externalizing disorders (e.g., aggressive behavior), and internalizing disorders (e.g., depression).[1] One factor or variable that could help account for these variations is the marital dispute resolution process that divorcing parents participate in. Advocates of marital conflict mediation hypothesize that children whose parents mediated their separation or divorce will be better adjusted than children whose parents dissolved their marriage through participation in the adversarial process.[2]

This hypothesis rests on the following theoretical rationales. First, mediation makes a greater contribution toward preventing parental conflict through improved communication and increased awareness of the underlying causes of spousal conflicts. If and when conflicts do occur, spouses are more likely to resolve them in a positive (win-win) way through compromise. This is a way of resolving conflicts that spouses learn to apply during mediation sessions.

Second, mediation facilitates coparenting. Coparenting is in the best interests of both children and parents.

Third, mediation increases the level of compliance with child (and spousal) support arrangements because the spouses themselves are responsible for reaching the agreements in which these arrangements are described.

Evidence confirming or disconfirming these three hypotheses will be reviewed under the headings of *parental conflict, custody arrangements,* and *income deprivation.*

Parental Conflict

Evidence presented by a number of different researchers using different samples and covering different time periods indicates that parental conflict is associated with an increase in adjustment problems among children.[3] If divorce mediation moderates parental conflict and the adversarial process exacerbates it, then we should find differences in the adjustment of children of parents in mediated and adversarial groups.

One of the major hypotheses that Joan Kelly (1990b) tested in her study was that "divorce mediation would lead to fewer and less intense conflicts in the 2 years after divorce" (p. 12). Anticipating the possibility that this outcome simply reflected lower and less serious levels of marital conflict among mediation clients, Kelly measured marital conflict among mediation and adversarial clients. Parents in these groups reported similar levels of marital conflict. She found no differences in the frequency of overall conflict reported by ex-spouses in the mediation and adversarial groups 1 year after the divorce was granted. During this period, significant differences in the frequency of general conflict were reported by parents with and without minor-aged children. More specifically, parents with minor-aged children reported significantly higher levels of conflict.

The overall or general measure of conflict used by Kelly (1990b) was a composite measure that included a number of specific conflicts relating to "financial, visiting, custody, parenting and child rearing issues" (p. 12). Findings based on the use of these specific measures did reveal significant differences between parents in the mediation and adversarial groups. Compared with parents in the latter group, mediation parents reported significantly fewer conflicts over custody, access, and child support issues during the process itself and at the time of the final divorce. One year after the divorce, parents in the mediation group reported significantly fewer conflicts over communications related to the children.

No differences in the frequency of general or specific (child-related) conflict were reported by parents in the mediation and adversarial groups 2 years after the final divorce was granted. This finding is interpreted by Kelly as supporting the premise that "mediation mutes or reduces conflict hypotheses because parents in the mediation sample had significantly more contact and communication with each other than did parents in the adversarial sample" (p. 14). In other words, even though they had far more opportunities for conflict than adversarial parents, mediation parents reported similar levels of conflict.

One reason for this outcome may be the significantly lower levels of anger reported by parents in the mediation group. Because anger and conflict are positively correlated, lower levels of anger are likely to be associated with lower levels of conflict. Another possible reason is the significantly higher levels of cooperation reported by mediation parents (Kelly, 1990b). A similar finding is reported by Pearson and Thoennes (1988): They found parents who had successfully mediated their separations or divorces (i.e., reached full agreements) were significantly more cooperative at 1 year postdivorce than adversarial clients. As cooperation and conflict are inversely associated, higher levels of cooperation are likely to be associated with lower levels of parental conflict.

Unlike Kelly (1990b), Pearson and Thoennes (1988) did include measures of effects on children in their study. They found children's adjustment at 1 year postdivorce to be unrelated to parents' participation in mediation or the adversarial process. In other words, children of parents in the two groups were equally well adjusted (or poorly adjusted).

Taken together, these results suggest that marital conflict mediation makes a greater contribution toward reducing the level of parental conflict than the mediation process, but this does not make a significant difference to the adjustment of children in the mediation and adversarial parent groups. In interpreting the findings that support this conclusion, it is important to remember that Kelly did not actually measure child adjustment and to note that the Pearson and Thoennes (1988) study has a number of problems that could have influenced their findings. First, a relatively weak version of divorce mediation was being compared with regular adversarial processing. Thus, mediation parents in the three family courts participated in an average of only 2.2 mediation sessions. In two of the three courts, children did not participate in them. According to Pearson and Thoennes, the mediation they studied was "a brief process that typically did not require the child's direct participation" (p. 293). The adversarial process, on the other hand, was not described as being especially brief, and an unknown number of lawyer participants in the process adopted a conciliatory, mediatorlike role.

Second, some evidence indicates that the minimum time for measuring child adjustment following divorce is 5 years; Pearson and Thoennes's findings are based on a postintervention period of 12 to 15 months.[4]

Third, the total effect of a marital dispute resolution process on child adjustment requires statistical (or qualitative) analyses of its direct *and* indirect effects. The latter tend to be ignored, even though their salience is recognized. Thus, Pearson and Thoennes (1988) note that "the effects of the [mediation or the adversarial] process will be most felt by parents, and . . . children will benefit only indirectly through the enhanced well-being of parents" (pp. 293-294).

The mechanisms through which the enhanced well-being of parents influences the well-being of children have been identified by a number of scholars who, unfortunately, have not included participation in marital conflict resolution process as a variable.[5] We have included it in a parent conflict effects model that describes the direct and indirect ways through which parent conflict could influence children's adjustment (Figure 11.1).

In this model, the marital dispute resolution process (mediation or adversarial process) is hypothesized to have a variety of indirect effects on the adjustments of children. In one set of linkages, mediation reduces the level of parental conflict and increases parental cooperation. Through imitation (modeling effect), children learn to be more cooperative and less conflictual in their relations with others. Less conflictual and cooperative parents are more likely to share coparenting responsibility for socializing, supporting, and controlling their children. Less conflictual and more cooperative parents are also likely to experience lower levels of stress and are therefore more likely to operate as caring, responsible coparents.

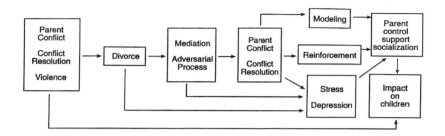

Figure 11.1. Parental Conflict Model

When parental conflicts do occur, mediation parents are more likely to resolve them through compromise. Compromise is more likely than coercion to produce win-win solutions. This outcome reinforces compromising parental behavior and facilitates responsible, caring coparenting. The same contingencies apply to children who imitate the conflict-resolving strategies used by their parents, and who are then reinforced or rewarded for solving conflicts through compromise.

Mediation may also have indirect effects that adversely influence children's adjustment. Thus, mediation is more likely than the adversarial process to be associated with depression among women (Emery & Wyer, 1987b). This decreases the likelihood of effective coparenting. Ineffective coparenting has a negative effect on children's adjustment.

In addition to modeling, reinforcement, stress, and depression, divorce and predivorce (marital) levels of conflict and violence, as well as ways of resolving conflicts, are hypothesized to have direct effects on children's adjustment. Although we have not included them, findings from a number of studies suggest that the cognitions of children and adolescents also mediate the effect of parental conflict on them (Grych & Fincham, 1990).

The model described in Figure 11.2 is not a fully developed one because we have not identified the specific aspects or domains of children's adjustment that are influenced by the mediating variables included in it. Modeling and reinforcement, for example, may be

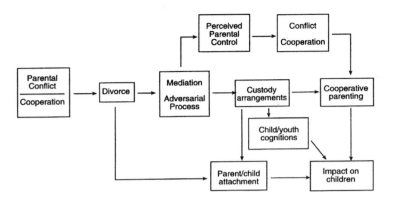

Figure 11.2. Custody Arrangements Model

associated with externalizing disorders and stress with internalizing disorders (Forehand, Neighbours, Devine, & Armistead, 1994). Again, the same mediating variable (e.g., coercive ways of resolving conflicts), may have different effects on adolescents, depending on their cognitions (Grych & Fincham, 1990). In addition, *interactions* between the mediating variables and age, sex, and time span (postdivorce) are important but cannot be included in a nonrecursive (linear model). Clearly, tests for interactions should be undertaken in statistical analyses of the data (Buehler, Krishnakumar, Anthony, Tittsworth, & Stone, 1994; Emery, 1982; Forehand et al., 1994). Last, remarriage is not included in the model, even though it has a significant effect on children's adjustment and may vary with participation in mediation or the adversarial process (Hetherington, 1993; Hetherington, Arnett, & Hollier, 1988).

Custody Arrangements

The starting point for our description and evaluation of research on the effects of custody arrangements on children's adjustment is the link between marital dispute resolution processes and custody arrangements. In this connection, Pearson and Thoennes (1988) found mediation and joint custody arrangements to be strongly associated. Thus, joint custody arrangements were reported by 70% of mediation parents and 30% of adversarial parents. Ellis (1995) found that 69% of 200 divorced parents in two family courts were granted sole custody, and approximately 8% were granted joint custody. Most of those who were awarded joint custody were awarded joint legal custody (7.0%). More than 85% of those who were awarded sole custody were women.

Mediators in one of the courts studied by Ellis (1994) did not use the terms *joint and sole custody* and *visitation or access*. Instead, they talked about *shared parenting*. Shared parenting patterns varied between one in which children spend an approximately equal amount of time in the houses of both parents who share legal responsibility for them, to one in which the children stay with one of the parents during alternating weekends and on one night during the week. Common to all shared parenting patterns was the designation of one parent's home as the children's primary residence and that parent as the primary caretaker. A comparison of parenting patterns reported by mediation and adversarial parents revealed that the former came closer toward realizing the goal of shared parenting (as measured by the duration, frequency, and quality of nonprimary caretaker-child contacts) than parents who participated in the adversarial process.[6]

In interpreting these findings, it is relevant to discover the degree to which joint custody arrangements reflect the bias of mediators and the preferences of both parents.[7] Mediators do appear to prefer joint custody but so do some separating or divorcing parents. Pearson and Thoennes (1984), for example, found that 22% of mediating parents and 5% of adversarial parents already had joint custodial arrangements in place prior to their participation in one or the other of these marital dispute resolution processes. Lawyers prefer sole custody and so do many adversarial clients (Ellis, 1994). With respect to both mediation and the adversarial process, then, custody arrangements reflect the influence of self-selection, mediator and lawyer preferences, and the process itself. The independent, additive, or interactive contribution of these factors to custody arrangements has not been published in any of the studies we reviewed.

Evidence has been published by Koel, Clark, Phear, and Hauser (1988) linking joint custody arrangements with "post divorce stress and dissatisfaction in . . . families" (p. 85). Following Hetherington and

Camara (1984), they used relitigation rates as an indicator of family problems. Based on their analyses of court records on 479 sole custody cases and 199 joint custody cases, they found no differences in relitigation rates between parents in the two custody groupings. This finding surprised them for two reasons. It was not consistent with that of Ilfeld, Ilfeld, and Alexander (1982) who found lower relitigation rates among joint custody parents or their "clinical impressions of families with joint custody as being more cooperative and less litigious" (p. 86).

These findings are interesting and may be relevant to child adjustment, but children's adjustment was not directly measured by Koel et al. (1988). One of the few studies that did measure both custody arrangements and child behavior problems was conducted by Kitzmann (1993).

Kitzmann's (1993) sample consisted of 61 families "who requested child custody hearings from a . . . domestic relations court one year earlier" (p. 3). Subjects were asked at random to participate in either mediation or the adversarial process. Following a procedure adopted by Pearson and Thoennes (1988), the youngest child was the target child whose adjustment was measured using the Achenbach Child Behaviour Checklist for children aged between 4 and 16 years or the Eyberg Child Behavior Inventory for children aged 2 or 3 years. Parental conflict and depression were also measured.

Physical custody was granted to almost all of the parents in both the mediation and adversarial samples. Joint legal custody was granted to only a few more parents in the mediation sample. On the basis of this description of joint custody arrangements, we may conclude that mediation and adversarial parents did not differ significantly in their joint custody arrangements.

The theoretical rationale for mediation had led Kitzmann (1993) to predict that children of mediation parents would show fewer behavioral problems. This hypothesis was not confirmed. She found no difference in the frequency of behavior problems among children in the mediation and adversarial parent groups.

One possible reason for Kitzmann's finding is the level of parental conflict over visitation reported by the few mediation parents with joint physical custody arrangements who remarried during the year. In addition to the effects of remarriage (see Hetherington et al., 1988), one or both of these parents may not have preferred joint physical custody, but the mediator may have persuaded them that it was in their best interests as well as the best interests of the children. Next, because joint custody arrangements are more complex and require a greater amount of cooperation between parents, they are more difficult to work out in the short run (i.e., during the first postprocessing year) than sole custody arrangements. Joint physical custody arrangements, then, are unlikely to facilitate cooperative, caring coparenting when parents with relatively high conflict levels do not want them. Under these conditions, joint physical custody may increase the likelihood of child adjustment problems.

Last, measurement error may play a part in accounting for Kitzmann's finding of no differences in adjustment among children in the mediation and adversarial parent groups. She relied exclusively on parents for information on the behavior problems of their children and she also reports that there was more parent conflict over visitation in the mediation sample. Such parents, especially those who did not want joint custody arrangements in the first place, may be more willing to report more problems with respect to custody or visitation arrangements they want to change.

A more general caveat applies to research on the effects of child custody arrangements in which researchers assume that the labels used to identify custody arrangements in court records and questionnaires administered to divorced parents (e.g., sole custody, joint legal custody, joint physical custody, split custody) accurately describe actual parent-child visiting patterns. Often they do not (Clark, Whitney, & Beck, 1988; Koel et al., 1988). Ellis (1995) found qualitative evidence indicating substantial variations *within* as well as *between* differently labeled custody arrangements. Moreover, the effect of any specific custody arrangement on parents as well as parental reports of children's adjustment varies with gender and the length of time during which the arrangement was in place.

We conclude this segment by noting that scholars whose work we reviewed did not publish studies linking marital dispute resolution process, custody arrangements, *and* child adjustment. We attempt to do this in the custody arrangements effects model described in Figure 11.2.

In this model, custody arrangements have only indirect effects on children's adjustment. That is to say, they influence children's adjustment through their effects on cooperative, caring parenting; maintaining child-parent attachment; and parental conflict and cooperation.

Income Deprivation

In Canada, sole custody is granted to women in 70% of all divorces and to men in approximately 8% of them (Statistics Canada, 1990). Figures published by Statistics Canada (1992) also indicate that women earn approximately two thirds of the income of men in all occupational categories. Under a legal principle of self-sufficiency, divorced women (and men) are expected to become economically self-sufficient. This means that child and spousal support levels must not be set at levels that are adequate for the needs of mothers and their children but that decrease the single parent's motivation to become self-sufficient. This set of conditions has led Pask (1993) to conclude that one "primary consequence of divorce is . . . a serious disparity in economic circumstances: . . . men largely maintain the same standard of living as they had before marriage, whereas the women and children live in poverty" (p. 187).

Divorced fathers could reduce the economic disparity between themselves and their former wives by complying with social norms (e.g., parental responsibility, equity) that motivate them to regularly make child support payments exceeding the levels set by the court. At a minimum, they could regularly make the child support payments ordered by the court.[8] Among the reasons cited by them for doing neither is that (a) their income levels are so low they cannot afford to, (b) why should they, when their ex-wives make it so difficult for them to get together with their children,[9] and (c) divorce is a package deal in which the severance of spousal ties also means the severance of ties between "dumped" husbands and their children (Ellis, 1994; Furstenberg & Cherlin, 1991; Pearson & Anhalt, 1994; Seltzer & Brandreth, 1994).

Evidence presented by Stroup and Pollock (1995) indicates that the average income of divorced women is 22% lower than the average income of married women. The comparable figure for divorced versus married men is 10%. Divorced men earn significantly less than married men in all socioeconomic status categories. On the basis of these findings, which came from a relatively large survey by the National Opinion Research Centre of 1,500 English-speaking adults aged 18 years and over, Stroup and Pollock conclude that "divorced men are not as able to pay as Weitzman's (1985) study would indicate" (p. 53).[10] Income deprivation among divorced wives and mothers, then, may be associated with income deprivation among divorced husbands and fathers.

Out of 10 divorced spouses, 7 remarry. Among them are many divorced male partners who either remarry or become involved in a cohabiting relationship (Vanier Institute of the Family, 1994). The incomes of an unknown number of these men may not drop—they may even increase after divorce—but the number of children who need to be supported increases. The end result is the same. They may not be able to afford to support their own children or stepchildren from a new marriage or relationship as well as the children of their prior marriage(s) because a larger number of children from different families are competing for the same economic resources. Findings from a number of studies indicate that child support decreases following remarriage of the non-custodial (usually male) parent (Hetherington & Camara, 1984; Wallerstein & Huntington, 1983). Here, normative and economic factors combine to maintain disparities in the economic situation of divorced husbands and wives.

The single most important factor accounting for economic deprivation of divorced wives and mothers is their level of economic deprivation during their marriages. Based on the results of a comparative study of divorced and married women, Morgan (1991) reached the following conclusion: "To a large extent, economic circumstances following the departure from marriage depend on characteristics and decisions that shaped the woman's life long before the marriage ended" (p. 96). Income deprivation among married mothers and wives, then, is strongly associated with income deprivation among divorced mothers and wives.[11]

Pearson (1991) included both the earning capacity of women prior to the divorce and the marital dispute process in her study of the financial status of divorced wives and mothers. One of her major findings was that women's earning capacity and the number of dependent children they were responsible for were more significant determinants of their postdivorce financial status than their participation in mediation or the adversarial process.

In interpreting Pearson's findings, it is again relevant to note that the women in her sample who participated in mediation participated in a weak, court-based version of it. Thus, she reports being distressed by the fact that "30% of women . . . reported that the process was rushed and needed more time" (p. 194). A rushed mediation process does not facilitate full financial disclosure or the use of independent appraisers. Moreover, a rushed process aimed at achieving the court (bureaucratic) objective of handling the largest number of cases at the lowest cost requires a fairly high degree of mediator control over the mediation process. Expedited case processing and a high degree of mediator control may adversely influence the financial position of divorced women and their children.

A high degree of mediator control adversely influences the financial status of divorced women and children through its effect on the payment of child support and visitation. The research findings of Braver, Wolchik, Sandler, Fogas, and Zvetina (1991) indicate that noncustodial parents who saw themselves as having control over the divorce process and its outcomes were more likely to make their child support payments regularly and on time. In their research on the association between child support and child access, Pearson and Anhalt (1992) found that problems with child support payments were a better predictor of access problems than access problems were of child support problems. These authors also suggest that both child support problems and access problems reflect "more basic conflict about economic matters" (p. 107). Compared with the adversarial process, mediation makes a greater contribution to reducing parental conflict, including economic conflict, and should therefore facilitate greater compliance with child support and access arrangements.[12]

To this point, we have identified a number of factors that influence the level of economic deprivation among divorced mothers generally and among divorced mothers who participated in the mediation or the adversarial process in particular. Economic deprivation influences child adjustment directly through material deprivation (e.g., inadequate food, clothing, housing, health care) and indirectly through its tendency to increase stress, which in turn decreases the effectiveness of parenting

(Colletta, 1983; McLanahan & Garfinkel, 1993; Starrels, Bould, & Nicholas, 1994).

In concluding this segment, we note again the prevalence of research studies in which the marital dispute resolution process is not included as a variable. It is included in the income deprivation model described below (Figure 11.3). In this model, income deprivation indirectly affects children's adjustment through its influence on stress, material deprivation, and child/youth cognitions.

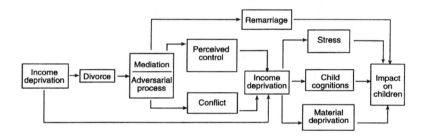

Figure 11.3. Income Deprivation Model

Summary of Findings

Parental Conflict

The adjustment of minor-aged children is more strongly associated with postdivorce parental conflict than is participation in either mediation or the adversarial process.

Postdivorce parental conflict varies inversely with participation in mediation or the adversarial process, with parents having higher levels of contact reporting levels of conflict similar to those reported by adversarial parents having lower contact.

Differences in levels of conflict reported by mediation and adversarial parents vary inversely with the time span since final divorce, with lower levels of conflict being reported by the former during the 1st year and similar levels of conflict between parents in the two groups being reported by the end of the second year.

Postdivorce levels of cooperation vary with participation in mediation or the adversarial process, with mediation parents reporting higher levels of cooperation than adversarial parents 2 years following the final divorce.

At 2 years postdivorce, mediation and adversarial parents reported similar levels of conflict and equally well adjusted (or poorly adjusted) children.

Custody Arrangements

Custody arrangements vary with participation in mediation or the adversarial process, with a significantly higher proportion of mediation parents participating in joint custody and a significantly higher proportion of adversarial parents (mainly mothers) being awarded sole custody.

At 1 year after divorce, children's behavior problems do not vary with participation in either mediation or the adversarial process when mediation and adversarial parents participate in similar custody arrangements.

Income Deprivation

Postdivorce income levels of divorced mothers and fathers vary with their predivorce income levels; the higher the level of predivorce income, the higher will be the postdivorce level of income.

Differences in predivorce income levels favoring fathers are reflected in differences in postdivorce income levels favoring fathers.

Divorce is associated with a drop in income for both mothers and fathers, with the drop being significantly greater for mothers with custody of children.

When predivorce income levels are taken into account, there are no significant differences in the postdivorce financial statuses of mothers who participated in mediation or the adversarial process.

Conclusions

▓ The passage of time has a more significant effect on the adjustment of children of divorced parents than participation in mediation or the adversarial process.

- Child custody arrangements have a more significant effect in the short run on the adjustment of children than participation in mediation or the adversarial process.
- Income deprivation has a more significant effect on the adjustment of children than participation in mediation or the adversarial process.
- Partial research designs and poor measurements of child custody arrangements and child adjustment make it difficult to draw valid conclusions about marital dispute resolution process effects on children's adjustments that are mediated by parental conflict or custody arrangements.

Notes

1. Boys tend to be more aggressive (Forgatch, Patterson, & Skinner, 1988; Hetherington, 1979; Rutter, 1971; Wallerstein & Kelly, 1980), whereas girls tend to be more depressed, withdrawn, and anxious (Emery, 1982; Hetherington, Cox, & Cox, 1982). The findings of Smetana, Yau, Restrepo, & Braeges (1991) suggest that children's adjustment may be better in divorced families with low parental conflict than in married families with high parental conflict.

2. See Coogler, Weber, and McKenry (1979), Irving (1980), and Milne (1978).

3. See Amato (1993), Buehler et al. (1994), Camara and Resnick (1988), Emery (1982), and Forehand et al. (1994).

4. The effect of divorce on the adjustment of children appears to vary with time and one of its correlates, the developmental level of the children. See Hetherington et al. (1982), Kalter (1987), and Wallerstein, Corbin, and Lewis (1988). Some researchers report that the effects of divorce and participation in mediation or the adversarial process work themselves out with a 2-year postdivorce (postprocessing) period of time; others report finding "negative consequences for adolescents which last for at least several years" (Forehand et al., 1994, p. 392).

5. The model described in this figure is an inductively derived one that relies heavily on the work of Amato (1993), Camara and Resnick (1988), Dodge (1990), Downey and Coyne (1990), Emery (1982), Emery and Wyer (1987b), Forgatch et al. (1988), Hetherington (1993), Kelly (1990a), Patterson (1986), Peterson and Zill (1986), and Rutter (1971).

6. A recent decision by the Ontario Court of Appeal permits custodial parents to move out of the court's jurisdiction taking the children with them, regardless of the wishes of noncustodial parents or how well they fulfilled their parental obligations (Fine, 1995). Some of the likely consequences of this decision are identified by Elster (1990).

7. See Francis (1981) and Pask (1993).

8. Estimates of proportions of divorced fathers who make no payments, late payments, or irregular payments vary between 30% and 70%. See Cassetty (1983), Pask and McCall (1989), and Taylor (1984).

9. Their own safety as well as the safety and well-being of their children motivate some mothers to avoid contact with noncustodial fathers. See Pearson and Anhalt (1992).

10. The findings of Hoffman and Duncan (1988) and Okin (1991) also contradict those presented by Weitzman (1985).

11. For reviews of economic and other consequences of divorce, see Kitson and Morgan (1990) and Rowe (1991).

12. For a good discussion of the economic, relational, moral (normative), and punitive factors accounting for variations in compliance with child support orders, see Chambers (1979).

References

Alexander, J., Giesen, B., Munch, R., & Smelser, N. (1987). *The micro-macro link*. Los Angeles: University of California Press.

Amato, P. (1993). Children's adjustment to divorce: Theories, hypotheses and empirical support. *Journal of Marriage and the Family, 55*, 23-38.

American Behavioral Scientist, 36. (1994). Entire issue.

Anonymous. (1995, Fall). The gender gap: International survey. *Medical Post*, 16-18, 73.

Attorney General. (1989). *Report of the Advisory Committee on Mediation in Family Law*. Toronto: Ministry of the Attorney General.

Bantz, B. (1991). Divorce mediation: For better or worse? *Mediation Quarterly, 22*, 51-60.

Benjamin, M., & Irving, H. (1993). Toward a feminist-informed model of therapeutic family mediation. *Mediation Quarterly, 10*, 129-149.

Berkowitz, L. (1978). Is criminal violence normative behavior? Hostile and instrumental aggression in violent incidents. *Journal of Research in Crime & Delinquency, 15*, 148-181.

Berkowitz, L. (1982). Aversive conditions as stimuli to aggression. In L. Berkowitz (Ed.), *Advances in experimental social psychology* (Vol. 15, pp. 249-288). Orlando, FL: Academic Press.

Berkowitz, L. (1993). Toward a general theory of anger and emotional aggression: Implications of the cognitive-neoassociationistic perspective for the analysis of anger and other emotions. In R. S. Wyer & T. K. Srull (Eds.), *Perspectives on anger and emotion* (pp. 1-46). Hillsdale, NJ: Lawrence Erlbaum.

Bethel, C. A., & Singer, L. P. (1982). Mediation: A new remedy for cases of domestic violence. *Vermont Law Review, 7*, 15-32.

Blood, R. O., & Wolfe, D. (1960). *Husbands and wives: The dynamics of married living.* New York: Free Press.

Blumberg, R. L., & Coleman, M. T. (1986). A theoretical look at the gender balance of power in the American couple. *Journal of Family Issues, 10,* 225-250.

Blume, T. (1993). Update on systematic practice. *Mediation Quarterly, 11,* 195-197.

Bograd, M. (1984). Family systems approaches to wife battering: A feminist critique. *American Journal of Orthopsychiatry, 54,* 558-568.

Bograd, M. (1988). Feminist perspectives on wife abuse: An introduction. In K. Yllo & M. Bograd (Eds.), *Feminist perspectives on wife abuse* (pp. 11-26). Newbury Park, CA: Sage.

Bottomley, A. (1984). Resolving family disputes: A critical review. In M. Freeman (Ed.), *State, law and the family: Critical perspectives* (pp. 293-303). London: Tavistock.

Bowker, L. (1983). *Beating wife-beating.* Lexington, MA: D. C. Heath.

Braver, S. H., Wolchik, L., Sandler, S. A., Fogas, N., & Zvetina, D. (1991). Frequency of visitation by divorced fathers: Differences in reports by fathers and mothers. *American Journal of Orthopsychiatry, 61,* 448-454.

Brinkerhoff, M., & Lupri, E. (1988). Interspousal violence. *Canadian Journal of Sociology, 13,* 407-434.

Brockman, J., & Chunn, D. (Eds.). (1993). *Investigating gender bias.* Toronto: Thompson.

Buehler, C., Krishnakumar, A., Anthony, S., Tittsworth, S., & Stone, G. (1994). Hostile parental conflict and youth maladjustment. *Family Relations, 43,* 409-416.

Bush, R. A., & Folger, J. (1994). *The promise of mediation.* San Francisco, CA: Jossey-Bass.

Camara, K., & Resnick, G. (1988). Interparental conflict and cooperation: Factors mediating children's post-divorce adjustment. In S. A. Wolchik & P. Karoly (Eds.), *Children of divorce: Empirical perspectives on adjustment* (pp. 169-195). New York: Gardner.

Carnevale, P. J., & Pruitt, D. (1992). Negotiation and mediation. *Annual Review of Psychology, 43,* 531-582.

Cassetty, J. (Ed.). (1983). *The parental-child support obligation.* Lexington, MA: Lexington Books.

Cavanagh, R., & Rhode, D. (1976). The unauthorized practice of law and *pro se* divorce: An empirical analysis. *Yale Law Journal, 86,* 104.

Chafetz, J. (1980, September). Conflict resolution in marriage: Toward a theory of spousal strategies and marital dissolution rates. *Journal of Family Issues,* 397-421.

Chambers, D. L. (1979). *Making fathers pay.* Chicago: University of Chicago Press.

Chesler, P. (1986). *Mothers on trial: The battle for children and custody.* Orlando, FL: Harcourt Brace.

Children's Law Reform Act, 1990, § 31(1), Ontario, Canada.

Clark, S., Whitney, R., & Beck, J. (1988). Discrepancies between custody arrangements and practices: *De jure* and *de facto* custody. *Journal of Divorce, 11,* 219-238.

Cobb, S. (1992, June). *The domestication of violence in mediation: The social construction of disciplinary power in law.* Paper presented at the Law and Society annual meeting, Philadelphia, PA.

Colletta, N. (1983). Stressful lives: The situation of divorced mothers and their children. *Journal of Divorce 6,* 19-31.

Comeaux, E. A. (1983). A guide to implementing divorce mediation in the public sector. *Conciliation Courts Review, 21,* 1-25.

Coogler, O. J., Weber, R., & McKenry, P. (1979). Divorce mediation: A means of facilitating divorce and adjustment. *The Family Coordinator, 28,* 255-259.

Crawford, M., & Gartner, R. (1992). *Woman killing: Intimate femicide in Ontario, 1974-1990.* Toronto: Women We Honour Action Committee and the Ontario Women's Directorate.

Cromwell, R., & Olson, D. (1975). *Power in families.* New York: John Wiley.

Cromwell, V., & Cromwell, R. E. (1978). Perceived dominance in decision-making and conflict resolution among anglo, black and Chicano couples. *Journal of Marriage and the Family, 40,* 749-759.

Davis, A., & Salem, R. (1984). Dealing with power imbalances in the mediation of interpersonal disputes. In J. A. Lemmon (Ed.), *Procedures for guiding the divorce mediation process* [Special issue]. *Mediation Quarterly, 6.*

Davis, G. (1980a). Mediation in divorce: A theoretical perspective. *Journal of Social Welfare Law, 6,* 130-135.

Davis, G. (1980b). *Research to monitor Bristol courts family conciliation service.* Bristol, UK: University of Bristol, Department of Social Administration.

Davis, G. (1983). Conciliation and the professions. *Family Law, 13,* 6-10.

Davis, G., & Bader, K. (1983). *In-court mediation on custody and access issues: The Filer Study.* Bristol, UK: University of Bristol, Department of Social Administration.

Davis, G., & Roberts, M. (1989). Mediation and the battle of the sexes. *Family Law, 18,* 305-306.

Depner, C., Cannata, K., & Ricci, I. (1994). Client evaluations of mediation services: The impact of case characteristics and mediation service models. *Family and Conciliation Courts Review, 32,* 306-325.

Deutch, M. (1949). A theory of cooperation and competition. *Human Relations, 2,* 129-152.

Deutch, M. (1973). *The resolution of conflict.* New Haven, CT: Yale University Press.

Deutch, M. (1994). Constructive conflict resolution: Principles, training, research. *Journal of Social Issues, 50,* 13-32.

Divorce Act of 1985, § 9(2), Ottawa, Canada.

Dobash, R. E., & Dobash, R. P. (1992). *Women, violence and social change.* London: Routledge.

Dobash, R. E., Dobash, R., Wilson, M., & Daly, M. (1992). The myth of sexual symmetry in marital violence. *Social Problems, 39,* 71-91.

Dobash, R. P., & Dobash, R. E. (1979). *Violence against wives: A case against the patriarchy.* New York: Free Press.

Dodge, K. (1990). Developmental psychopathology in children of depressed mothers. *Developmental Psychology, 26,* 835-845.

Domestic Abuse Intervention Project. (1984). Domestic Abuse Intervention Project: The power-control wheel. Duluth, MN: Author.

Downey, G., & Coyne, J. (1990). Children of depressed parents: An integrative review. *Psychological Bulletin, 108,* 50-76.

Dunford, F., Huizinga, D., & Elliott, D. (1990). The role of arrest in domestic assault: The Omaha police experiment. *Criminology, 28,* 183-205.

Dutton, D. G., & Browning, J. (1988). Concern for power, fear of intimacy and aversive stimuli for wife abuse. In G. T. Hotaling, D. Finkelhor, J. T. Kirkpatrick, & M. Strauss (Eds.), *Family abuse and its consequences* (pp. 163-175). Newbury Park, CA: Sage.

Easteal, P. (1993). *Killing the beloved: Homicide between adult sexual intimates.* Canberra, Australia: Australian Institute of Criminology.

Edwards, A. (1987). Male violence in feminist theory: An analysis of the changing conceptions of sex/gender violence and male dominance. In J. Hanmer & M. Maynard (Eds.), *Women, violence and social control.* (pp. 13-29). Atlantic Highlands, NJ: Humanities Press.

Eisenberg, M. A. (1982). The bargain principle and its limits. *Harvard Law Review, 95,* 741-801.

Ellis, D. (1990). Marital conflict mediation and post separation abuse. *Law and Inequality, 8,* 317-339.

Ellis, D. (1993). Family courts, marital conflict resolution and wife assault. In Zoe Hilton (Ed.), *Legal responses to wife assault.* (pp. 165-187). Newbury Park, CA: Sage.

Ellis, D. (1994). *Family mediation pilot project.* Toronto: Attorney General of Ontario.

Ellis, D. (1995). *Custody, access and support arrangements in family courts: A pilot study.* Ottawa, Canada: Department of Justice.

Ellis, D., & DeKeseredy, W. (1989). Marital status and woman abuse: The DAD model. *International Journal of Sociology of the Family, 19,* 67-87.

Ellis, D., & Dekeseredy, W. (1995). Homicide and femicide. In D. Ellis & W. Dekeseredy, *The wrong stuff: An introduction to the sociological study of crime and deviance.* Toronto: Allyn & Bacon.

Ellis, D., & Stuckless, N. (1992). Pre-separation abuse, marital conflict mediation and post-separation abuse. *Mediation Quarterly, 9,* 205-226.

Ellis, D., & Wight, L. (1995). *Gender asymmetry in marital and post-separation violence.* Unpublished manuscript.

Elster, J. (1990). *Solomonic judgements: Studies in the limitations of rationality.* Cambridge, UK: Cambridge University Press.

Elster, J. (1991). *Nuts and bolts for the social sciences.* New York: Cambridge University Press.

Emery, R., & Wyer, M. (1987a). Child custody mediation and litigation: An experimental evaluation of the experience of parents. *Journal of Consulting and Clinical Psychology, 55,* 179-186.

Emery, R., & Wyer, M. M. (1987b, May). Divorce mediation. *American Sociologist,* 472-480.

Emery, R. E. (1982). Interparental conflict and children of discord and divorce. *Psychological Bulletin, 92,* 310-330.

Enns, C. Z. (1988). Dilemmas of power and equality in marital and family counseling: Proposal for a feminist perspective. *Journal of Counseling and Development, 67,* 242-247.

Family Law Act, 1990, § 3(1), Ontario, Canada.

Faulk, M. (1974, July). Men who assault their wives. *Medicine, Science and the Law,* 180-183.

Felstiner, W., Abel, R., & Sarat, A. (1980-81). The emergence and transformation of disputes: Naming, blaming and claiming. *Journal of Legal Pluralism, 19,* 1-16.

Fine, S. (1995, June 24). Ruling leaves dads out in cold. *Toronto Globe and Mail,* pp. 56-67.

Fischer, K., Vidman, N., & Ellis, R. (1993). The culture of battering and the role of mediator in domestic violence cases. *SMU Law Review, 46,* 2117-2174.

Fisher, R., & Ury, W. (1981). *Getting to yes: Negotiating agreement without giving in.* Boston: Houghton Mifflin.

Folberg, J. (Ed.). (1986). *Joint custody and shared parenting*. Madison, WI: Association of Conciliation and Family Courts, Bureau of National Affairs.

Folberg, J., & Taylor, A. (1984). *Mediation: A comprehensive guide to resolving conflicts without litigation*. San Francisco: Jossey-Bass.

Forehand, R., Neighbours, B., Devine, D., & Armistead, L. (1994). Interparental conflict and parental divorce: The individual, relative and interactive effects on adolescents across four years. *Family Relations, 43,* 387-393.

Forgatch, H., Patterson, G., & Skinner, M. (1988). A mediational model for the effect of antisocial behavior in boys. In S. A. Wolchik & P. Karoly (Eds.), *Children of divorce: Empirical perspectives on adjustment* (pp. 135-153). New York: Gardner.

Francis, P. (1981). Divorce and the law and order lobby. *Family Law, 11,* 69-73.

Freud, S. (1948). *Group psychology and the analysis of the ego*. London: Hogarth.

Frontenac Family Referral Service. (1980). *Violent couples II*. Kingston, Ontario: Author.

Frontenac Family Referral Service. (1984). *Couples in crisis II*. Kingston, Ontario: Author.

Furstenberg, F., & Cherlin, A. (1991). *Divorced families: What happens to children when parents part*. Cambridge, MA: Harvard University Press.

Galanter, M. (1981). Justice in many rooms: Courts, private ordering and indigenous law. *Journal of Legal Pluralism, 1,* 19-28.

Gardner, D. (1981). Study of court conciliation services. In *Couples in crisis II* (pp. 43-47). Kingston, Ontario: Frontenac Family Referral Service.

Giles-Sims, J. (1983). *Wife-beating: A systems theory approach*. New York: Guilford.

Gondolf, E. W. (1988). Who are those guys? Toward a behavioral typology of batterers. *Violence and Victims, 3,* 187-203.

Gondolf, E. W., & Fisher, E. R. (1988). *Battered women as survivors: An alternative to treating learned helplessness*. Lexington, MA: Lexington Books.

Griffiths, J. (1986). What do Dutch lawyers actually do in divorce cases? *Law and Society Review, 20,* 135-175.

Grillo, T. (1991). The mediation alternative: Process dangers of women. *The Yale Law Journal, 100,* 1545-1610.

Grych, J. H., & Fincham, F. (1990). Marital conflict and children's adjustment. *Psychological Bulletin, 108,* 267-290.

Gulliver, P. H. (1979). *Disputes and negotiations: A cross-cultural perspective*. New York: Academic Press.

Hamberger, L. K., & Hastings, J. E. (1985). Personality correlates of men who abuse their partners: A cross-validation study. *Journal of Family Violence, 1,* 323-341.

Hamner, J. (1978). Violence and the social control of women. In G. Littlejohn, B. Smart, J. Wakeford, & N. Yuval-Davies (Eds.), *Power and the state* (pp. 27-36). London: Croom Helm.

Hamner, J., & Maynard, M. (1987). Violence and gender stratification. In J. Hanmer and M. Maynard (Eds.), *Women, violence & social control* (pp. 1-12). Atlantic Highlands, NJ: Humanities Press.

Haynes, J. (1981). *Divorce mediation: A practical guide for therapists and counselors*. New York: Springer.

Haynes, J. (1988). Power balancing. In J. Folberg & A. Milne (Eds.), *Divorce mediation: Theory and practice* (pp. 276-295). New York: Guilford.

Haynes, J. (1992). Mediation and therapy: An alternate view. *Mediation Quarterly, 10,* 21-32.

Hershon, M., & Rosenbaum, A. (1991). Over vs. undercontrolled hostility: Application of the construct to the classification of mortally violent men. *Violence and Victims, 6,* 151-158.

Hetherington, E. M. (1979). Divorce: A child's perspective. *American Psychologist, 34,* 851-858.

Hetherington, E. M. (1993). An overview of the Virginia longitudinal study of divorce and remarriage with a focus on early adolescence. *Journal of Family Psychology, 7,* 39-56.

Hetherington, E. M., Arnett J., & Hollier, E. D. (1988). Adjustment of parents and children to remarriage. In E. M. Hetherington & J. D. Arastesh (Ed.), *Impact of divorce, single parenting and step-parenting on children.* Hillsdale, NJ: Lawrence Erlbaum.

Hetherington, E. M., & Camara, K. (1984). Families in transition: The process of dissolution and reconstruction. In R. Parke (Ed.), *Review of Child Development Research* (Vol. 7, pp. 398-439). Chicago: University of Chicago Press.

Hetherington, E. M., Cox, M., & Cox, R. (1982). Effects of divorce on parents and children. In N. Lamb (Ed.), *Non-traditional families: Parenting and child development* (pp. 233-285). Hillsdale, NJ: Lawrence Erlbaum.

Hillary, M., & Johnson, J. (1985). Selection and evaluation of attorneys in divorce cases involving minor children. *Journal of Divorce, 9,* 93-104.

Hirschel, J. D., Hutchinson, I. W., & Dean, C. (1992). The failure of arrest to deter wife abuse. *Journal of Research in Crime and Delinquency, 29,* 7-31.

Hoffman, S., & Duncan, G. (1988). What are the economic consequences of divorce? *Demography, 24,* 641-645.

Holtzworth-Monroe, A., & Stuart, G. (in press). Typologies of male batterers: Three subtypes and the differences between them. *Psychological Bulletin.*

Hopper, J. (1992, August). *Oppositioned roles in divorce: Bringing order and meaning to the dissolution process.* Paper presented at the annual meeting of the American Sociological Association, Pittsburgh, PA.

Huber, J., & Spitze, G. (1983). *Sex stratification: Children, housework and jobs.* New York: Academic Press.

Ilfeld, F., Ilfeld, H., & Alexander, J. (1982). Does joint custody work? A first look at outcome data on relitigation. *American Journal of Psychiatry, 139,* 62-66.

Irving, H. (1980). *Divorce mediation: A rational alternative to the adversary system.* New York: Universe.

Irving, H., & Benjamin, M. (1984). A study of conciliation in the family court of Toronto: Implications for socio-legal practice. In J. M. Eekelaar & S. N. Katz (Eds.), *The resolution of family conflict* (pp. 268-295). Toronto: Butterworth.

Johnston, J., & Campbell, L. (1993). A clinical typology of interparental violence in dispute-custody divorces. *American Journal of Orthopsychiatry, 63,* 190-199.

Jones, A. (1994). *Next time she'll be dead: Battering and how to stop it.* Boston: Beacon.

Journal of Criminal Law and Criminology, 83(1). (1992). Entire issue.

Kalter, N. (1987). Long-term effects of divorce on children: A developmental vulnerability model. *American Journal of Orthopsychiatry, 57,* 587-600.

Kelly, J. (1990a). Is mediation less expensive? A comparison of mediated and adversarial divorce costs. *Mediation Quarterly, 8,* 16-26.

Kelly, J. (1990b, December). *Mediated and adversarial divorce resolution processes: An analysis of post-divorce outcomes.* Final report prepared for the Fund for Dispute

Resolution. Available from the Northern California Mediation Center, 100 Tamal Plaza, Corte Madera, CA 94925.

Kelly, J., & Gigy, L. (1989). *Divorce mediation: Characteristics of clients and outcomes.* In K. Kressel, D. Pruitt, & Associates (Eds.), *Mediation research: The process and effectiveness of third party intervention* (pp. 263-283). San Francisco, CA: Jossey-Bass.

Kelly, L. (1987). The continuum of sexual violence. In J. Hanmer & M. Maynard (Eds.), *Women, violence and social control* (pp. 46-60). Atlantic Highlands, NJ: Humanities Press

Kennedy, L., & Dutton, D. (1989). The incidence of wife assault in Alberta. *Canadian Journal of Behavioural Science, 21,* 40-54.

Kitson, G., & Morgan, L. (1990). The multiple consequences of divorce. *Journal of Marriage and the Family, 52,* 913-924.

Kitzmann, V. (1993, March). *Child outcomes one year following mediated and litigated child custody disputes.* Paper presented at the Anniversary Meeting of the Society for Research in Child Development, New Orleans, LA.

Koel, A., Clark, C., Phear, W., & Hauser, B. (1988). A comparison of joint and sole legal custody arrangements. In S. A. Wolchik & P. Karoly (Eds.), *Children of divorce* (pp. 73-89). New York: Gardner.

Koel, A., Clark, S., Straus, R., Whitney, R., & Houser, B. (1994). Patterns of prelitigation in the postdivorce family. *Journal of Marriage and the Family, 56,* 265-277.

Kressel, K., Butler-DeFreitas, F., Forlenza, S., & Wilcox, C. (1989, Summer). Research in contested custody mediation: An illustration of the case study method. *Mediation Quarterly* (pp. 67-83).

Kressel, K., Deutch, M., Jaffe, N., Tuchman, B., & Watson, C. (1977). Mediated negotiation in divorce and labor disputes. A comparison. *Conciliation Courts Review, 15,* 1-12.

Kressel, K., Frontera, E., Forlenza, S., & Butler, F. (1994). The settlement-orientation vs. the problem-solving style in custody mediation. *Journal of Social Issues, 50,* 67-83.

Kressel, K., Jaffe, N., Tuchman, C., Watson, C., & Deutch, M. (1980). A typology of divorcing couples: Implications for mediation and the divorce process. *Family Process 15,* 9-12.

Kressel, K., & Pruitt, D. (1989). Conclusion: A research perspective on the mediation of social conflict. In K. Kressel, D. Pruitt, & Associates (Eds.), *Mediation Research: The Process and Effectiveness of Third Party Intervention,* (pp. 394-435). San Francisco, CA: Jossey-Bass.

Kressel, K., Pruitt, D., & Associates (Eds.). (1989). *Mediation Research: The process and the effectiveness of third party intervention.* San Francisco, CA: Jossey-Bass.

Kritzer, H. (1990). *The justice broker: Lawyers and ordinary litigation.* New York: Oxford University Press.

Lazarus, R. S., & DeLongis, A. (1983, March). Psychological stress and coping in aging. *American Psychologist,* 245-254.

Lerman, L. (1984). Mediation of wife abuse cases: The adverse impact of informal dispute resolution on women. *Harvard Women's Law Journal, 7,* 57-113.

Libow, J., Raskin, P., & Caust, B. (1982). Feminist and family systems theory: Are they irreconcilable? *American Journal of Family Therapy, 10,* 3-12.

Lupri, E. (1990). Male violence in the home. In C. McKie & K. Thompson (Eds.), *Canadian social trends.* Toronto: Thompson.

Mahoney, M. R. (1991). Legal images of battered women: Redefining the issue of separation. *Michigan Law Review, 90,* 1-94.

Margolin, F. (1973). *An approach to the resolution of visitation disputes post-divorce: Short-term counselling.* Unpublished doctoral dissertation, United States International University, San Diego, CA.

Margolin, G., Sibner, L., & Gleberman, L. (1988). Wife battering. In V. B. Van Hasselt, R. L. Morrison, A. S. Bellack, & M. Hersen (Eds.), *Handbook of family violence* (pp. 89-117). New York: Plenum.

Martin, D. (1976). *Battered wives.* New York: Pocket Books.

McDonald, G. W. (1980). Family power: The assessment of a decade of theory and research. *Journal of Marriage and the Family, 42,* 841-854.

McIsaac, H. (1996). The divorce revolution: A critique. *California Family Law Report, 10,* 3069-3072.

McLanahan, S., & Garfinkel, J. (1993). Single mothers in the United States: Growth, problems and policies. In J. Hudson & B. Galaway (Eds.), *Single parent families* (pp. 15-30). Toronto: Thompson.

McLindon, J. (1987). Separate but unequal: The economic disaster for women and children. *Family Law Quarterly, 2,* 351-408.

Mercy, J., & Saltzman, L. (1989). Fatal violence among spouses in the United States 1976-1985. *American Journal of Public Health, 79,* 595-599.

Milne, A. (1978). Custody of children in a divorce process: A family self-determination model. *Conciliation Courts Review, 16,* 1-10.

Mnookin, R. (1979, February). *Bargaining in the shadow of the law: The case of divorce* (Working paper #3). University of California, Berkeley, School of Law.

Monahan, J. (1981). *The clinical prediction of violent behavior.* Washington, DC: U.S. Government Printing Office.

Morgan, L. (1991). *After marriage ends: Economic consequences for mid-life women.* Newbury Park, CA: Sage.

Neumann, D. (1992). How mediation can effectively address the male-female power imbalance in divorce. *Mediation Quarterly, 9,* 227-240.

O'Gorman, H. (1963). *Lawyers in matrimonial cases.* Glencoe, IL: Free Press.

O'Leary, K. D. (1993). Through a psychological lens: Personality traits, personality disorders and levels of violence. In R. Gelles & D. Loseke (Eds.), *Current controversies on family violence* (pp. 7-30). Newbury Park, CA: Sage.

Ogus, A. (1991). *The costs and effectiveness of divorce mediation.* Manchester, UK: University of Manchester, Faculty of Law.

Ogus, A., Walker, J., & Jones-Lee, M. (1989). *The costs and effectiveness of conciliation in England and Wales.* Report prepared for the Lord Chancellor by the Conciliation Project Unit, University of Newcastle Upon Tyne, England.

Okin, S. (1991). Economic equality after divorce. *Dissent, 38,* 383-394.

Ontario Association of Interval and Transition Houses. (1989, November). *Stop violence against women* (Background report). Toronto: Author.

Pagelow, M. D. (1993). Justice for victims of spouse abuse in divorce and child custody cases. *Violence and Victims, 8,* 69-80.

Parkinson, L. (1983). Conciliation: Pros and cons II. *Family Law, 13,* 183-186.

Pask, E. D. (1993). Family law and policy in Canada: Economic implications for single custodial mothers and their children. In J. Hudson & B. Galway (Eds.), *Single parent families* (pp. 185-201). Toronto: Thompson.

Pask, E. D., & McCall, M. (Eds.). (1988). *How much and why? The economic implications of marriage breakdown: Spousal and child support.* Calgary, Canada: Canadian Institute for Law and the Family.

Patterson, G. R. (1986, April). Performance models for antisocial boys. *American Psychologist,* 432-444.

Pearson, J. (1991, Winter). The equity of mediated divorce agreements. *Mediation Quarterly,* 179-197.

Pearson, J., & Anhalt, J. (1992, May). *The enforcement of visitation rights: A preliminary assessment of five exemplary programs.* Paper presented at the Annual Meeting of the Law and Society Association, Philadelphia, PA.

Pearson, J., & Anhalt, J. (1993). When parents complain about visitation. *Mediation Quarterly, 11,* 139-156.

Pearson, J., & Anhalt, J. (1994). Examining the connection between child access and child support. *Family and Conciliation Courts Review, 32,* 93-109.

Pearson, J., & Thoennes, N. (1984). Mediating and litigating custody disputes: A longitudinal evaluation. *Family Law Quarterly, 17,* 497-524.

Pearson, J., & Thoennes, N. (1988). Mediating parent-child postdivorce arrangements. In E. M. Hetherington & J. D. Arasteh (Eds.), *Impact of divorce, single parenting and stepparenting on children.* Hillsdale, NJ: Lawrence Erlbaum.

Pearson, J., & Thoennes, N. (1989). Divorce mediation: Reflections on a decade of research. In K. Kressel, D. Pruitt, & Associates (Eds.), *Mediation research: The process and effectiveness of third-party intervention* (pp. 9-30). San Francisco, CA: Jossey-Bass.

Pearson, J., Thoennes, N., & Vanderkooi, L. (1982). The decision to mediate: The profiles of individuals who accept and reject the opportunity to mediate contested child custody and visitation issues. *Journal of Divorce, 6,* 17-35.

Peterson, J. L., & Zill, N. (1986). Marital disruption, parent-child relationships and behavior problems in children. *Journal of Marriage and the Family, 48,* 295-307.

Pierson, R., & Cohen, M. (1994). *Strong voices.* Toronto: Lorimer.

Pruitt, D., Pierce, R., Millicuddy, H., Welton, G., & Castrianno, L. (1993). Long term success in mediation. *Law and Human Behavior, 17,* 313-330.

Radford, J. (1992). Introduction. In J. Radford & D. Russell (Eds.), *The politics of woman killing* (pp. 3-13). New York: Twayne.

Ricci, J. (1985). Mediator's notebook: Reflections on promoting equal empowerment and entitlement for women. *Journal of Divorce, 8,* 79-92.

Richardson, C. J. (1988). *Court-based divorce mediation in four Canadian cities.* Ottawa, Canada: Department of Justice.

Rifkin, J. (1984). Mediation from a feminist perspective: Promise and problems. *Law & Inequality, 21,* 330-342.

Roberts, M. (1992). Systems or selves? Some ethical issues in family mediation. *Mediation Quarterly, 10,* 3-19.

Rosenthal, D. (1974). *Lawyer and client: Who's in charge?* New York: Russell Sage.

Rowe, B. R. (1991). The economic consequences of divorce: Findings from seven states. *The Journal of Divorce, 14,* 5-17.

Rubin, J. (1994). Models of conflict management. *Journal of Social Issues, 50,* 33-45.

Rutter, M. (1971). Parent-child separation: Psychological effects on children. *Journal of Psychology and Psychiatry, 12,* 233-260.

Sarat, A., & Felstiner, W. (1986). Law and strategy in the divorce lawyer's office, *Law and Society Review, 20,* 16-27.

Saunders, D. (1993). Husbands who assault: Multiple profiles. In Zoe Hilton (Ed.), *Legal responses to wife assault* (pp. 9-36). Newbury Park: Sage.

Scanzoni, J. (1965). A note on the sufficiency of wife responses in family research. *Pacific Sociological Review, 8,* 109-115.

Scanzoni, J. (1982). *Sexual bargaining: Power politics in the American marriage.* Chicago: University of Chicago Press.

Schechter, S. (1982). *Women and male violence: The visions and struggles of the battered women's movement.* Boston: South End.

Schelling, T. C. (1960). *The strategy of conflict.* London: Oxford University Press.

Schwartz, M. (1988). Marital status and woman abuse theory. *Journal of Family Violence, 3,* 239-248.

Schwartz, M. (1989). Asking the right questions: Battered wives are not all passive. *Sociology Viewpoints, 5,* 46-51.

Seltzer, J., & Brandreth, Y. (1994). What fathers say about involvement with children after separation. *Journal of Family Issues, 15,* 49-77.

Sherman, L. (1992). *Policing domestic violence: Experiments and dilemmas.* Toronto: Maxwell-Macmillan.

Sherman, L., & Berk, R. (1984). The specific deterrent effect of arrest for domestic assault. *American Sociological Review, 49,* 261-271.

Silbey, S., & Merry, S. (1986). Mediator settlement strategies. *Law and Policy, 8,* 7-32.

Simmel, G. (1955). *Conflict* (K. Wolff, Trans). Glencoe, IL: Free Press.

Smetana, J., Yau, J., Restrepo, R., & Braeges, R. (1991). Adolescent-parent conflict in married and divorced families. *Developmental Psychology, 27,* 1000-1010.

Smith, M. (1987). The incidence and prevalence of wife abuse in Toronto. *Violence and Victims, 2,* 33-47.

Smith, M. (1990). Sociodemographic risk factors in wife abuse: Results from a survey of Toronto women. *The Canadian Journal of Sociology, 15,* 39-58.

Somer, R. (1994). *Male and female perpetuated partner abuse: Testing a diathesis model.* Unpublished doctoral dissertation, University of Manitoba, Canada.

Somer, R., Barnes, G., & Murray, R. (1992). Alcohol consumption, alcohol abuse, personality and female perpetuated spouse abuse. *Personality and Individual Differences, 13,* 1315-1323.

Stallone, D. (1984). Decriminalization of violence in the home: Mediation in wife battering cases. *Law and Inequality, 2,* 493-519.

Stanko, E. A. (1987). Typical violence, normal precaution: Men, women and interpersonal violence in England and Wales. In J. Hanmer & M. Maynard (Eds.), *Women, violence and social control* (pp. 122-134). Atlantic Highlands, NJ: Humanities Press.

Starrels, M., Bould, S., & Nicholas, L. (1994). The feminization of poverty in the United States. *Journal of Family Issues, 15,* 590-607.

Statistics Canada. (1990). *Current demographic analyses: New trends in the family.* Ottawa, Canada: Ministry of Supply and Services.

Statistics Canada. (1992). *Earnings of men and women.* Ottawa, Canada: Ministry of Supply and Services.

Straus, M. (1973). A general systems theory approach to a theory of violence between family members. *Social Science Information, 12,* 105-112.

Straus, M. (1989). *Gender differences in assault in intimate relationships: Implications for the primary prevention of spousal violence.* Paper presented at the annual meeting of the American Society of Criminology, Reno, Nevada.

Straus, M. (1990). The conflict tactics scales and its critics: An evaluation and new data on validity and relativity. In M. Straus & R. Gelles (Eds.), *Physical violence in American families: Risk factors and adaptation to violence in 8,145 families* (pp. 49-73). New Brunswick, NJ: Transaction Books.

Straus, M., & Gelles, R. (1990). *Physical violence in American families: Risk factors and adaptation to violence in 8,145 families.* New Brunswick, NJ: Transaction Books.

Stroup, A. L., & Pollock, G. (1994). Economic consequences of marital dissolution. In C. A. Everett (Ed.), *The economics of divorce: The effects on parents and children* (pp. 37-54). New York: Haworth.

Stulberg, J., & Bridenback, M. (1981). *Citizen dispute settlement: A mediator's manual.* Tallahassee: Supreme Court of Florida.

Taylor, C. (1984). Making parents believe: The conditioning of child support and visitation rights. *Columbia Law Review, 84,* 1058-1088.

Thibaut, J., & Kelley, H. (1965). *The social psychology of groups.* New York: John Wiley.

Turk, J., & Bell, N. (1972). Measuring power in families. *Journal of Marriage and the Family, 34,* 215-222.

Vanier Institute of the Family. (1994). *Profiling Canada's families.* Ottawa: Author.

Walker, L. (1979). *The battered woman.* New York: Harper & Row.

Wallerstein, J., Corbin, S., & Lewis, J. (1988). Children of divorce—A ten-year study. In S. Wolchik & P. Karoly (Eds.), *Children of divorce* (pp. 197-213). New York: Gardner.

Wallerstein, J., & Kelly, J. (1980). *Surviving the break-up: How children and parents cope with divorce.* New York: Basic Books.

Watson, M., & Morton, T. (1983). *Mediation as an alternative to social study in child custody disputes.* Unpublished evaluation report of the family court of the First Circuit Court, Honolulu, Hawaii.

Weiner, N., & Gunderson, M. (1990). *Pay equity: Issues, options and experiences.* Toronto: Butterworth.

Weitzman, L. (1985). *The divorce revolution.* New York: Free Press.

Wilson, M., & Daly, M. (1994, March). Spousal homicide [Special issue]. *Juristat, 14*(8).

Yllö, K. (1993). Through a feminist lens: Gender, power and violence. In R. Gelles & D. Loseke (Eds.), *Current controversies on family violence* (pp. 47-62). Newbury Park, CA: Sage.

Index

About the Authors

Desmond Ellis is Chair of the Department of Sociology at York University, Ontario, Canada. He also serves on the Executive Committee of the La Marsh Research Centre on Violence and Conflict Regulation, which he helped to create in 1981. Prior to coming to York in 1974, he was Assistant Professor in the Department of Sociology at the University of North Carolina (UNC), Chapel Hill. While at UNC, he completed a study of violence in the North Carolina prison system. In 1984, he completed a longtitudinal study on the effects of marital violence, divorce mediation, and lawyer negotiations on separating couples. He earned his B.A. in sociology at the University of Leicester, England, an M.A. in sociology from McMaster University, Hamilton, Ontario, Canada, and his Ph.D. at Washington University, St. Louis, MO. His doctoral dissertation was an experimental study of violence among hyperkinetic children. His next research project will be a field experimental study of the effects of power imbalances on the process and outcomes of divorce mediation.

Noreen Stuckless is a member of the research science staff in the Department of Psychiatry at Mount Sinai Hospital, Toronto, Canada.

She has participated in the research and publication of a number of studies involving the effects of mediator and lawyer-based negotiations in separation and divorce. Her main area of research concerns violence— in particular, spousal violence and its causes and effects. She is completing her Ph.D. in Social Psychology at York University and has been awarded a 2-year Social Science Research Council postdoctoral fellowship in the Department of Psychiatry at the University of Toronto to examine the effects of postassault events on victims of violence. This research will be conducted in collaboration with the Joint Programme in Society, Women, and Health at Women's College Hospital and the Clarke Institute of Psychiatry.